HARD CUDDLES

Published by Melbourne Books
Level 9, 100 Collins Street,
Melbourne, VIC 3000
Australia
www.melbournebooks.com.au
info@melbournebooks.com.au

Title: Hard Cuddles: James 'The Hammer' Harding
Author: James 'The Hammer' Harding
ISBN: 9781925556261

A catalogue record for this book is available from the National Library of Australia

HARD CUDDLES

JAMES 'THE HAMMER' HARDING

M

MELBOURNE BOOKS

I dedicate this book to my sister, Elles.
One of the strongest and most supportive women in my life.

FOREWORD

The famous philosopher Joseph Campbell discovered that in every great story there is a hidden 'hero's journey'. It can be found in *The Wizard of Oz*, *Star Wars* and *The Matrix*, just to name a few. It goes like this: the hero starts out in a normal situation and gets shunted out into a world of uncertainty and turmoil. They find a teacher or make friends who point them in the right direction. Ultimately, they slay the proverbial dragon, only to discover that the dragon was inside of them all along. After the victory and the self-realisation, the journey ends with the hero's triumphant return home to tell the story.

James 'The Hammer' Harding has lived a full life. There is scarcely a stone he hasn't turned over, scarcely a fear that he hasn't tackled. He has lived a life full of both dreams and nightmares that we would probably have trouble distinguishing if we were in his shoes. With rules being broken at every turn, this story seems unreal to us readers. Though it may seem like a villain's journey, you will find a hero in these pages, in this man.

He has slayed the dragon but only after staring it in the eyes and taming it.

I have had the pleasure of spending a lot of time with James, initially while he was still driving the sword into the heart of the beast. When we met he had already decided to tame it and stopped believing its ruse, but he was still wrestling with how to finish the job. I am honoured to be his friend, to know his story and, most importantly, to have connected to the man that was born out of it.

While it may be hard at times to see it through the excesses that are outlined, this is truly a story about all of us but experienced in a way that only this man and few others could survive. If, on your life's journey, you haven't broken the rules that the Hammer has broken, here is your chance to live in his world for a few moments and dare to think whether you would've dealt with it in the same way—enjoy.

Equal parts naughty, bodacious and irrepressible, this full circle life story is about one of our true Wizards of Aus. With the balls that 'The Hammer' showed in his life it might have taken even more to tell this story.

Nice work mate! Proud of you and glad to call you my friend.

Trevor Hendy AM

INTRODUCTION

'Just a young gun with a quick fuse
I was uptight, wanna let loose
I was dreaming of bigger things
And wanna leave my own life behind
Not a yes sir, not a follower
Fit the box, fit the mold
Have a seat in the foyer, take a number
I was lightning before the thunder'
— Thunder, Imagine Dragons

What's not to like? Imagine you're twenty and you roll up to the best night clubs, bars and restaurants in town with your entourage. The queue is four deep and wraps around the corner but you walk past everyone and straight to the front, shaking hands and hugging the door guy and bouncers. You know them all because you looked after them with party favours. You linger out the front long enough so everyone can see you and your crew. Then straight inside, no paying. No need.

Once you're inside you're the rock star that everyone wants to know. It's all eyes on you. You hit the toilets to freshen up, then it's dance floor time. Sex, drugs and hardcore techno.

In the social circle you keep there are convicted criminals, gangsters, hit men, bikies, socialites, politicians, minor celebrities, CEOs, lawyers, high profile AFL administrators, street-level junkies and the mentally unstable. A melting pot of unmitigated chaos; it might mean one night you're front row at the kickboxing with Michael Kroger and Ann Peacock or in the commission flats at Kensington collecting debt money.

And women, so many women. A lot of these women I am referring to come from privileged backgrounds, went to excellent schools and grew up in the best areas. It's like they are drawn to the rough life—the bad boys—they found the whole scene intoxicating. Fair enough too, the best hotels and high-end cocaine all for the taking, it would be hard to say no. These women were fantastic but instantly replaceable. Most of them knew this but came along for the ride anyway.

What I can say is that life was never dull, there was always action. Not for the faint-hearted, this style of living, because it can all change in an instant. Momentum can shift very quickly. I found myself at rock bottom and I mean rock bottom.

You see, I have always been an addict. There are no half measures with me, it's full bore or not at all. This when mental illness and things like addiction were not really understood. So I didn't have much of an idea of why I couldn't pump the brakes. Believe me, there were times I would have liked to. I heard Ben Cousins' counsellor describe addiction as an out of control train with an inability to stop. You deal with it on a day-to-day basis. You might wake up with the best intentions. You promised yourself this was the last time, this was it, no more, you have had your fill, it would be madness to continue, you're going to sort your life out once and for all, enough of this carry on, you're a grown man, an adult, you can beat this. Then that little devil on your shoulder will whisper sweet nothings like, 'Hey pal, you know what? You have been really good for the last forty-five minutes, how about we celebrate?' The good voice will be defiant: 'No, no, no, you're on a roll here'. But that seductive devil always packages his idea so provocatively, the rotten motherfucker. 'Hey champ, you can always quit tomorrow, The Lobster has an ounce of the killer gear, pure. Imagine that first line, the chemical taste dripping down the back of your neck from your nasal passage, drip, drip, then the hairs on the back of your neck stand up, sounds good, eh?' I start fantasising about it, my stomach turns into a washing machine full of butterflies at the thought of getting on, it's too much to bear. Next thing I know I've rung The Lobster and somehow I'm driving to his house on autopilot. Fuck. I want to turn the car around but I have no control over it.

It is soul destroying, being controlled like that, knowing you don't have the willpower to defeat a substance, even if you wanted to. You fool yourself that you can quit when you want to, but deep down you know damn well it has you by the balls. When you get on, you have fleeting moments of clarity; you might be able to transport yourself to a happy moment from the past. For me it was always my childhood, I would go to happier days at the beach or on holidays up north, always with my family. I would be overwhelmed with the happiness I had experienced a long time ago. Then as close as it was, it would wear off and the dark abyss would engulf my being like a pack of hyenas. More, I would need more, anything to keep that feeling at bay, even for another sliver of time.

There are thousands of stories like mine: a middle-class kid from a respectable family who starts experimenting with drugs, gets in way over his head and falls through the cracks. But this story is different. This story is about how the kid claws his way back out.

BEING DIFFERENT

'To live is the rarest thing in the world. Most people exist, that is all.'
— Oscar Wilde

It has always been obvious to me that I am different to most other people I have met. It's like I am drinking water from a completely different well. As a young bloke it was a lot harder—I did cop it a bit for being different. Not enough for me to change though, I wasn't interested in fitting in.

I was only interested in learning subjects I had considered important. To this day I still can't do basic mathematics or read a clock, it's never interested me. But if I need to work something out mathematically for a business deal or anything to do with fishing, I don't have a problem.

No matter how much emphasis parents and teachers put on doing well at school, it didn't have any importance for me. Being a solid human and trying to do the right thing was what mattered.

There were times in my life when I was consistently getting into trouble for the way I chose to live my life and it was tempting to give up and try to fit in. But I didn't and I am so thankful that I have endured. In the end, it's not about being right or wrong; it's about staying true to yourself. No matter how far you have to go on your journey in life, you can always find your way back home.

This book was written as a process of self-healing and an opportunity to look back and remember how far I've come. If anyone reads this and decides that I haven't covered a particular story the way they remembered—well, they are probably correct. Everyone has their own sense of reality and their memories will be different to mine.

This story is mine, no one else's. I have done my best to be as candid as I can. The truth is by far the most entertaining form of reality. There have been plenty of stories that cannot be told out of respect for my wife and children. There are also stories that can't be told because many people I used to know are still very active in that world. Just because I decided to leave doesn't mean I am going to sell out. Rules are rules after all. A few people have done this and it makes for some pretty exciting reading but I entered that game with my head held high and I can certainly leave it the way I found it, meaning: I'm right here if anyone wants to see me.

I only considered letting other people read this after my sister snuck onto the computer and read a chapter. She loved what she saw and suggested I get it published. If this book helps someone who is stuck or helps a parent gain insight into what their kids might be going through, that is enough for me. It was certainly a massive learning curve for both my parents. My lovely Mum discovered spirituality as a way of healing herself through the process. At the tail end of my journey into the dark side, I found spirituality and meditation as well. Because of this we have this special bond that has allowed me to communicate with my Mum on a level that I thought was only possible with drugs. I found that drugs heightened my senses towards the spiritual realm and opened my eyes to a much more involved existence.

It's amazing, the people you attract in life. I have been blessed to meet some of the most charismatic and energetic humans. I have also had the opportunity to meet some really challenging souls. Some that I have met have been vital to helping me understand myself. When you are face-to-face with a known hit man, for example, you learn to rely on your instincts and intuition. This is when you feel really alive. Your body and skin tingling. Your senses are heightened when you are operating on a second-to-second basis. You're right in the moment.

That's where I still like to operate from: that dark side of life. Navigating my way down into a dark cavern doesn't concern me one bit, not if I can find some truth that will enrich my life or help someone. I am right at home with addicts, the homeless, the mentally challenged and the downright nasty. For me that is but another reflection of the system, just the same as the incredible stories you hear about humans achieving amazing things. You need both energies to get the balance right. I like to learn about both—some people may consider it an ugly truth. I like to think of it as a kind of beautiful darkness.

This discovery was profound because I learned to trust and rely on these senses to guide me back home. *Where the Wild Things Are,* by Maurice Sendak, expresses this so well. A young boy, Max gets in trouble and his mum sends him to his room. There, he uses his imagination to go on a journey to where the wild things are. He sails over to the island where monsters live and becomes one of them. Max uses a special trick to tame them, then he dances and bares his claws and fangs with them well into the night. Eventually he becomes the king of the monsters. But after a while he tires and gets bored and decides to sail back home. When he does, the monsters tell him they will miss him too much and they don't want him to go. Max leaves anyway and when he gets home, he finds his dinner waiting for him and it's still warm.

This is the story of my life.

A MASSIVE BABY

'Are you ready for this?'

The scales read 12 pounds 3 ounces when they weighed me at Bethlehem Hospital, Caulfield on 1 April 1981. I was the size of a six-month-old baby. Mum told me I was very sick. I swallowed some crap at birth. It turns out this isn't uncommon and might even be considered good life experience. I overcame my early predicament and was doted on by my parents and grandparents. My mother is a kind and loving person but we are very similar people and would often annoy each other. Mum was trying to get me to kinder as early as possible. Not only was I a handful, I was one of those kids that was ready to socialise very early. My upbringing was full of Sri Lankan customs. Nanna and her Mum would often come over when I was sick or misbehaving. I instantly knew I had better tighten things up a bit when Nanna came over.

Mum told me I was playing up in the supermarket one day and she walked over to tell me off. I took the opportunity to throw myself on the floor and yell out, 'Please don't kick me'. I hope that gives you an idea of how cunning I could be at such a tender age. Mum got used to dealing with all sorts of behaviour from me. Once I got loose, went out the front and changed everyone's mail around in the street. By the time Dad got home from work, Mum had usually had enough. We had exhausted each other. Dad would tap in and Mum would jump in the car to go and get some peace and quiet.

Right from the beginning there were always two voices in my head: a good voice and a voice that was more fun and interesting. You don't have to be a doctor to work out which one I followed in life. It wasn't till my late twenties did I even consider that the good voice may be trying to help me. I'm fairly sure from some of the stories my mother tells me I was a spirited child, forever pushing the boundaries and pushing people into pools.

NANNA AND GRAMPS

'There is only one happiness in life, to love and be loved'
— George Sand

I can still smell their house. My earliest memories include them. My feelings towards these people cannot be described in words. The two of them were angels put on earth to make other people's lives easier. I hope everyone else has the same overwhelming feeling when they talk about their grandparents. Mine were amazing.

There were many times when I was in trouble as a little person and having Nanna and Gramps living in the next street was a chance to escape from it all. I was safe there.

Someone had given me an old suitcase and it was perfect for a toddler: there was enough room for a book, my teddy bear and another toy. This was neatly packed and on standby near my bedroom door. Any time I felt my mother was completely out of line with her decision making or punishment, I would grab the suitcase and off I went. It is fair to say, I spent a lot of time around at their place.

Their backyard was massive with a vegetable patch and all sorts of fruit trees in it. In the corner near his shed was Gramps' prized avocado tree, standing prouder than a honeymooner's dick. Gramps really put the hours into it. He would often go out there and just stare at it, very much the way my Dad stares at Colorbond roofs.

My grandparents were born in Ceylon, now the beautiful island of Sri Lanka. We are what you call *burghers*—or fair-skinned Sri Lankans with Dutch surnames, due to our Dutch heritage. Gramps used to tell me some amazing stories about his life in Ceylon. My grandparents had a unique way of communicating. They had a certain place where they would meet where there was a big piece of cardboard. My grandpa would write my Nanna love notes on the ground with a rock and cover it with the cardboard. Gramps was very good-looking and spoke three languages: Singhalese, English and Latin. A highly educated man, he had a really eccentric way and loved to talk to people about their lives and financial situations. If you walked past his house, he would demand to know what you brought him or how much you were earning. He thought this was the height of good humour—to put people on the spot. He had a Norton motorcycle and was quite the man about town. His brother, Gem, was an entrepreneurial businessman who started tourism in Ceylon. Gem got up to all sorts of illegal shit and at one point smuggled gold to and from India. Gem also owned some of the original hotels in that beautiful country. The other brother, Earl, was the strongest man in Ceylon. He worked on the railroads and was able to bend a coin over on itself with his thumb and forefinger. Earl was a hippie and back then often wore a flower in his hair. He was also an artist and did what he liked, wandering around the country to the beat of his own drum.

Gramps had an obsession with England and anything English: cars, clothes, the monarchy, he even followed the English cricket team. If we saw a Jag driving down the street, he would point at it and say 'tops'. Gramps took me to the TAB and showed me how to bet when I was about twelve. We spent a lot of time together and it was never boring.

Nanna, on the other hand, could be very fiery and had a habit of faking illnesses if things didn't go her way. Gramps was a tight-arse and they would always fight over money. You knew if you saw Gramps in his chair with his chin resting on his chest he was in the dog house. Nanna was the best cook; it didn't matter if there were two or twenty people around there for lunch, as there often was. Gramps was treated like a bloody king at lunchtime every day. He would go and sit himself at the head of his table and wait. Nanna would produce the most amazing curries and all the bits and pieces that accompanied it. You could smell it from down the street. There were always people there and Gramps would hold court. He was capable of talking on any topic, but his real passion was to talk nonsense and he was really talented at it. Nanna was always telling him off for talking crap. You see, the stars aligned for me, I was born just when Gramps retired. He was a very stressed out sort of character before that, from what I am told. I never got to see that side of him. Occasionally he would reverse the white Valiant Charger out and we would go for a drive. All this time spent with such a wordsmith helped me hone my communication skills and he would teach me how to speak like an adult. Gramps would also chat with me about adult topics: politics, finance and world news. He loved it when I shared my opinion.

One Sunday afternoon when I was at their house with my young cousins, we went next door to their neighbour's house. The neighbours weren't home, so I decided to destroy the joint. I started smashing pot plants and throwing things into their pool. My cousins joined in and we had a really good time. For some reason it didn't occur to us that we would be identified as the culprits. Later that week my parents questioned me and it was revealed that my cousins had accused me of being the ringleader, so I was given a sound thrashing. My cousins were very good at putting me in it.

Their mother had it in for me, she couldn't bear to think that her boys were capable of that sort of behaviour. So blaming me became a consistent theme when I was growing up.

Often Gramps would wander up to our primary school right on lunchtime to buy my sister and I whatever we wanted from the tuckshop. Gramps would ask us if one of our friends wanted something as well. It was hilarious—when the kids would see my Gramps coming towards the school, they ran after my sister and me, keen to forge a quick friendship. What a bunch of fuck-knuckles they were, sucking up to the two of us in a desperate play to get some sweets.

With most of Dad's side now passed away and him being an only child, I was raised with a proper Sri Lankan upbringing. This comes as a big surprise to most people, including my wife. It wasn't till I took her to a family party did she understand the full extent of how Sri Lankan I was.

My time spent with Gramps most definitely helped form strong communication patterns. He never spoke to me like a child. It was extremely enjoyable to be asked for my opinion by such an educated man. Gramps enjoyed telling anyone who would listen that I was going to be a politician.

THE BIG H

'Delay is the deadliest form of denial.'
— C. Northcote Parkinson

Mum was one of five and arrived by boat after three months at sea. She was five when she came over to Australia. Her sisters called her London Lady because Mum didn't continue with the immigrant concept of sticking with your own. She had lots of friends outside the family and this was challenging for her sisters. My mum was also naughty and had an addictive streak, like my good self. It wasn't till recently that Mum explained that she was expelled from her high school. She had a charmed childhood being the youngest. She was very tall and had beautiful coloured skin.

After Mum was expelled she attended a business college—this had been decided by my grandparents and her eldest sister. In her family, the eldest sister had a big say in things. Mum went on to marry a man who had been badly abused as a young boy. This young boy grew up and repeated those violent habits with my mother.

Mum's first marriage ended after her abusive husband was caught red-handed by Gramps. The man was then removed from the situation. I imagine it was a big deal. Being Catholic and divorced would have been very tricky. Enter my Dad.

Mum told me she needed to work through a lot to feel comfortable to love again. Counsellors and healers weren't around as much back then. So Mum had to get through this by herself and trusting men would have been a massive challenge.

From all reports Dad was a full-blown stalker. Picture Matt Dillon in *Something About Mary* and you're on the right track. Poor Mum was still very fragile from her previous marriage and you have my old man wolf whistling at her work. Mum used to hide behind poles when she saw Dad's Kingswood coming but that didn't stop him. He just used to pull over and say 'Is that you hiding there Trish? Jump on in.'

Their first date was a debacle. Dad overdid it on the scotch-and-cokes and spewed all the way home. What a mess. Apparently he had his head out the window, giving her the 'I'm not normally like this Trish'.

I have seen photos of the two of them in their day and they were a really cool-looking couple. Dad was a surfer, so he was always bronzed and Mum had the Sri Lankan tan going herself. They looked really happy and healthy. Dad saw a good thing in Mum and he wasn't going to miss out. Shows what a terrific judge of character he was. Thirty-nine years of marriage, three children and seven grandkids is not a bad return for effort.

Dad was born and raised in Northcote, a completely different area to what it is today. His dad, Big Al, served in the war in Papua New Guinea and loved a drink. Dad's mum, Claire, also loved a drink and between the two of them it was challenging. There was lots of love, but the effects of alcoholism can be disruptive for a young bloke trying to find his way in life.

Dad never complains about his upbringing. You can tell there is still genuine care and deep emotion for his parents. Apparently Big Al had a bit of the devil in him, like myself. He loved to hang out at the pub with his mates for too long, he loved a smoke, a beer and a bet. He was also a bit of ladies' man, very competent on the dance floor and generally just loved a good time. The only problem with people like Big Al and me is our capacity to enjoy ourselves is completely different to everyone else's.

Dad's greatest accomplishment was bucking the trend of alcoholism in our lineage. After doing some work around addiction, I found that the effects of war can be felt generations on and alcoholism is one of the reasons for this. When those men came home from war, there wasn't support for them. So they drank to dull the pain and yearned for the camaraderie. That stopped with Dad—there was no way his children were going to deal with what he had to. But sometimes addiction is like a wildfire: it can jump a whole generation and flare up in another one.

Dad was a decent sportsman; he was a handy leg-spin bowler and batsman. He once bowled a whole side out with figures of 10/41 in his local comp. Dad also played at Fitzroy U/19 when Gary Wilson and Kevin Murray were there. He played in the premierships with Northcote Park where I believe he was an undersized ruckman. His other passion is the Collingwood Football Club. Victoria Park was only a drop punt from his house and his pathological love of this club is something he passed onto me. Dad is an amazing character, his ability to love is immense and when he gets behind something, he does it with his whole heart. The Collingwood Football Club is richer with him to support them.

Surfing was his real passion, which is unique with him being a northern suburbs boy. He just yearned for the salt water, very much like myself. It's hard to put into words; a good mate of mine says emotion is the ocean. When he was 18 Dad came home from a weekend of surfing and his mother had passed away due to the effects of alcohol.

So it was just Dad and Big Al left. Dad was engaged to a girl very similar to my first serious girlfriend, her name was Jenny. She was a model and very attractive, she was also a drinker and didn't put the same emphasis on health and wellbeing as Dad. So when Mum came into Dad's life, the old man's focus shifted.

Mum fell in love with Dad, especially when she saw his house and met Big Al. Their house wasn't a dump, but it definitely wasn't a plush Camberwell-type arrangement. Mum loved that Dad was still house proud, even though it was humble.

When Mum met Big Al she was amazed at how affectionate he was for those times. He was always hugging and kissing Dad. Think about that for one second—Big Al was born in 1911 and he was a hugger and kisser, he was way ahead of his time. Dad was very much the parent and had to keep Big Al on a tight leash. Mum loved going to the pub with Big Al and this suited him perfectly. He was very proud to show his mates down at the Carters Arms Hotel his boy and his lovely new partner.

Mum and Dad married and Big Al sold the Northcote property to give them enough money to put a deposit on our house in McKinnon. He lived with them till he passed away of stomach cancer. Just before he passed, he told Mum that he could see her with three beautiful children. How amazing is that? That's exactly what Mum ended up having.

I would love to have met Big Al, I think we would have been a great combination down at the pub. He had this pool cue that he always used at his local. Dad managed to grab it when he passed away. They called him the master at the pool table. I had it framed with his service number, nickname and a few nice photos of him and Claire. It's a nice memory and a fitting tribute.

HEAVEN WITH FRIENDS LIKE THESE

'Growing apart doesn't change that fact, that for a long time we grew side by side; our roots will always be tangled. I'm glad for that.'
— Ally Condie

My first day of grade prep went like any other grade prep's: I walked in with my *Fraggle Rock* school bag and noticed the kid next to me had a *Fraggle Rock* school bag. We became best friends, simple as that. To this day I haven't had another friend like him.

Carlos is his name, as in Carlos the Jackal. This bloke always seemed to be able to give people the slip when he was in the gun. Carlos was of rich Albanian heritage, he had an awkward pear-shaped body, with shoulders like pier pylons and big child-bearing hips. Carlos had an unusual capsicum-shaped head and liked to wear his baseball caps backwards, still does. Carlos was a big tracksuit wearer. Carlos was very street smart, he was a little hustler from way back. Out of all the friends I have had in my life, this shifty prick is the bloke I love the most. We have been through so much together.

There was another guy called Slick. This bloke had a new identity every week. He was always trying some new look or style. Slick was a full-blown professional liar. Slick's mum and my mum were friends, so we became friends as well. The one thing about this peanut was that he really knew how to get under my skin.

One day he gave me the shits in class. He was what you call a habitual line-stepper. I told him I was going to whip his ass at playtime, the whole class heard about it. Everybody was amped. I sat there in class, took my windcheater off and started to tie a knot with one of the arms. I was trying to fashion a mace and chain. When the bell went we all ran out into the middle of the grounds. It was sunny and I moved Slick around, so the sun was directly in his eyes. Then I started whipping the shit out of him with my weapon. I gave Slick a good old-fashioned flogging. There were people all around us, not dissimilar to Russell Crowe in *Gladiator*. At least that's how I felt.

Slick had this ass-whooping coming for a long time, I whacked away at this prick until I backed him up onto the cyclone fence. Old Slick couldn't do a thing but lean up against the fence and wait till I was finished. He was crying like Nick Riewoldt. The only negative for me was that the ass-whooping was right in front of the teachers' lounge. These teachers had full view of my epic performance on the playground. I should have asked 'Are you not entertained?'

The loudspeaker roared, 'Can James Harding please come to the office?' All the kids started cheering and I threw a hand in the air. I was really working the crowd now and I started a slow jog back to the office. The crowd couldn't get enough as I exited the arena. Poor Slick was a crumpled mess, leaning up against the cyclone fence alone and crying.

I was a hyperactive individual who looked a lot like a skinny hamster. I had a bowl haircut like Moe from The Three Stooges. Mum thought the haircut made me look handsome, I was by far the naughtiest kid and was always getting in trouble for distracting the class. My concentration levels were that of a goldfish. I would easily get bored and start entertaining the classroom. Evidently my routine wasn't as appreciated by the teachers as some of my classmates and I would often end up in the principal's office. Now you would think as a mate, you would want to keep this news from parents. Oh no, not my friends. They couldn't wait to run out to my Mum and tell her what trouble I'd been up too.

So there was this dash that happened at my primary school every afternoon at 3:30. I would rush to the door to be the first person to leave class. My mum would either by waiting in the car or near the car and as soon as that bell went I would take off running, sprinting and shepherding my friends from Mum. If she was in the car I would start screaming at her as soon as I could see her, 'MUM, START THE CAR, LET'S GO, START THE CAR!' Or if Mum was standing near the car I would sprint and yell 'MUM, LETS GO, C'MON ENOUGH TALKING, LET'S GET OUT OF HERE!' Meanwhile as this is all going on, my mates are running behind me yelling 'MRS. HARDING, YOU SHOULD HAVE SEEN WHAT JAMES DID TODAY, MRS. HARDING.' No wonder I have trust issues, what the hell is that crap? Staunch crew, can you just imagine what Mum must have thought? What a bunch of give-ups.

To be fair I was always a bit different to the rest of the kids in my class. Things that 'normal' kids love doing like winning at sports and doing well academically never really interested me. Sure, I would happily participate if asked, but in truth it didn't really faze me whether I was included or not. My passion was conversing about life and nature, swimming in the sea, going on adventures, fishing, camping, and collecting bugs and insects. School did not interest me at all, it was just mundane, there was no excitement to it.

My sister and I were both very similar, a couple of misfits. We would often sit together to eat lunch. She understood. It wasn't as if we were outcasts. The other kids included us, we just thought differently. We were very deep emotional children. I can honestly say from grade six onwards was when all the other kids started to mature. Then we both really came into our own. But up until then it was a little lonely. But that was fine by me, I loved and still love my own company.

OAKLEIGH MACCAS BRICK DROP

'We cant be brave without fear.'
— Muhammad Ali

As a young fella, my Dad was always my hero. We have a very deep connection and the trust and understanding we have goes back many lifetimes. He is a good, strong man who prides himself on being honest and direct. I can rely on Dad and I have always felt safe with him.

One night we headed off to Maccas in Oakleigh. This was a huge deal because Maccas wasn't everywhere at this stage and families used to cook every night. So going out for dinner was big deal and, correct me if I'm wrong, but McDonald's used to taste good.

I shouldn't really remember this story at all, but my memory for some things is astonishing. As we got to Maccas, I went into the children's playground and Mum and Dad went to order. I remember playing away and then in came this slightly older kid. My senses went off and I started watching him.

This kid looked over to me and said 'You see that big rock over there?' and I said, 'Yes'. He told me he was going to smash it over my head. I won't ever forget the feeling of sheer terror as this kid walked over to the rock to pick it up. It was absolutely terrifying. I couldn't move, I couldn't scream, I couldn't do anything. I just stood there and waited for my fate at the hands of a psychotic juvenile at Oakleigh McDonald's.

As the kid made his way over to me, the playground door opened and a deep voice said, 'Where do you think you are going with that?' It was Dad. I immediately felt safe and knew everything was going to be okay. The kid dropped the rock and Dad came and gave me a cuddle. I remember being pretty shaken up. Dad has always been a super emotional and affectionate person, so when he hugs you, well, you stay hugged. As a child it was really wonderful to have a Dad around that cared, you just knew he was always going to be in your corner. His timing and his ability to make us all feel safe, carries him into the top echelon of fathers.

Can you imagine what could have happened if he was looking at Facebook or Instagram instead of watching me? I may not be writing this book.

ADDICTED AT 6 YEARS OLD

'Every form of addiction is bad, no matter whether the narcotic be alcohol or morphine or idealism.'
— Carl Jung

As early as I can remember I have had an insatiable addiction to any sort of mind-altering substance. In fact, I am easily addicted to anything: food, fun, alcohol, drugs, people, a good time, anything that gets the adrenaline pumping.

My earliest recollection of being addicted to drugs was in grade two. It was spring and a lovely sunny day. I have always suffered from asthma and on a couple of occasions it got quite serious. I always carried a Ventolin asthma puffer. On this particular day I was tearing around the playground when I noticed that I was short of breath. I had experienced this before and realised an asthma attack was not far off, so I immediately walked back to the school and made my way upstairs to the classroom.

When I found my bag hanging on its hook out the front of the classroom, I grabbed the Ventolin and took two puffs. Just above the row of hooks was a window that overlooked the whole playground. While I stood there and waited for the medication to work, I had a thought. What would happen if I continued to keep on puffing?

I held the Ventolin in my mouth and I continued to squeeze the pump over and over again. Call me crazy, but I had this overwhelming sense of excitement as to what was going to happen and that was when I slowly started to feel like I was stepping away from my body. It was full steam ahead. *Pssht, pssht, pssht*, I was pressing away. That's when I heard that magical word for the first time. *SFIDFIDA* is what it sounded like. That's the only way I can describe it. This sound came in waves from the left eardrum and moved into the right eardrum over and over again. That noise, *SFIDFIDA* was the direct result of hallucinating from taking too much Ventolin. I was well aware what I was doing was forbidden but I just could not stop. *Pssht, pssht, pssht*, I kept pressing, the *SFIDFIDA* got louder and more present. It felt like someone was singing straight through my head. In my mind it felt like I was watching myself, watching the kids running around the school playground and I can recall thinking, 'I bet they're not having as much fun as me.'

I was in such a peaceful state of mind. It was undoubtedly dangerous and I'm sure I knew this, but the issue of safety had never entered my mind, it still doesn't. My ability to always feel safe is part of my genetic make-up and is probably a massive part of the reason nothing sinister has really happened to me. That and a dash of good luck.

Pssht, pssht, pssht, now it seemed like I was getting further and further away from my body and the *SFIDFIDA* noise was getting more prominent. I realised it may be the time to just enjoy the fruits of my labour and continue my quest for the ultimate buzz at a later date. The Ventolin dropped down to my thigh with my hand attached to it. I felt like some sort of grand conductor standing on the second floor, directing and controlling with my mind the little school children down below, running around like ants.

My Ventolin puffing extravaganzas only subsided when Mum realised I was burning through these puffers at a rapid rate, she took me to see an asthma specialist, Dr McIntyre, one of the leading asthma men in Melbourne. He had the gall to question the regularity and administration of my application. If anything I was proactive, rather than overzealous. The two of them ganged up on me, the old divide and conquer routine. I had seen my school teachers try this on me. I held firm to my denial of the accusations against my good name, till the doc suggested that if one was to continue using Ventolin at this rate, one would risk the chance of getting emphysema. What the fuck? Now I was all for having a good time, but this startling revelation was too much. Still…the seed had been sown.

THE DOG BITE

'Don't let the same dog bite you twice.'
— Chuck Berry

It was a reasonably overcast day. My sister and I were playing in the front garden when Jerusalem Joe, our next door neighbour popped over to our house and asked my parents if I could go for a bike ride with him. Jerusalem Joe was fond of me and made a real effort to include me in his activities. He managed three daughters and I guess he considered me the little boy he longed for. Jerusalem Joe was a unique looking specimen, very much from the David Helfgott mould, the real life piano player that inspired the Oscar for Geoffrey Rush in the movie *Shine.*

Jerusalem Joe was a trailblazer in the fashion stakes as well. You would often see him tearing around Bentleigh in a pair of tracksuit pants, Velcro runners and a leather man-bag. Not the sort of man-bag you see the men of today carrying with the leather shoulder strap. This was more of a man-purse with a little leather strap that you put around your wrist. I was always amazed by his trendsetting bag. Once I filled in at Jerusalem Joe's company for a day and his employees all called him 'the enigma', due to his hyperactivity.

I was riding a hand-me-down BMX from one of my cousins. Dad had done it up with a new seat and hand grips to make it passable. In hindsight it was awful, but at the time I thought it was very special.

We were about a block away from our houses when we turned into Austin Street and I had a feeling as soon as I turned into the street, that something was not right. There were lots of people pottering around and then it happened.

Jerusalem Joe was about ten metres in front of me as we were halfway down the street and everything started to slow down. I heard a dog barking and a man yelling. I recall it was getting closer to me. I looked to see this grey blur coming towards me. Jerusalem Joe by this stage had stopped to look back at what was happening because this motherfucker was growling and making a godawful noise.

A grey weimaraner had charged out of its house and started attacking my calf. I felt my leg compress and I saw the dog shaking his head from side to side. It was as if time stood still, everyone was watching what was happening to me, but no one seemed to be able to do anything. It was all so quiet and serene. Very much like an out-of-body experience. I don't recall any pain. After the dog had bitten me, he raced off. I thought it might be a good idea to jump off my bike and see if there was any damage to my leg. Upon first inspection, everything looked okay as there was no damage to my track pants, not even a hole. I continued wearing them for years after the attack.

When I jumped off the bike, the situation hit me like a fishmonger's prices at Christmas. I sat down on the footpath and lifted up the track pant leg and saw that the dog had made an upside-down *u* shape incision on the whole of my calf. As I lifted my pant leg further, the bottom of the u-shaped skin flap had caught in the elastic and come off. So all I saw was bloody, pink flesh the size of the back of my calf. I knew then and there that this was one of those life changing moments.

People started screaming and running around not knowing what to do. One of my kinder friend's father happened to be working in the street and chased the dog with a shovel. As I sat there on the nature strip holding my calf to my leg, the owner of the dog ran out to me with some tea towels and started to secure them around my wound. I guess I was in shock because I didn't feel anything. But I remember being calm under pressure, a skill that would serve me well during my life. Blood started to seep through the first tea towel and drip onto the ground, so the owner wrapped another one around it.

I could see the fear in the dog owner's eyes, he was terrified. The man couldn't bring himself to say anything, he just stared at me. There was blood all over the footpath by this stage and poor old Jerusalem Joe had turned pale. He decided it would be best if he rode home to tell Dad. I recall people talking about an ambulance because of the blood loss. There was quite a crowd now and all of them where freaking out. I recall the sun setting at the bottom of the street as I watched for Dad's car.

Then he turned the corner in his white Falcon station wagon that he was so damned proud of. Such an overwhelming feeling of safety and relief washed over me. Everything was going to be all right now, even though my leg was torn apart and my calf was hanging by a piece of skin. I felt safe because Dad was there. He took charge and got me into the back seat straight away. I can't remember him saying much, he didn't need to. I knew he had the situation under control. That's a special feeling, an unwritten understanding between Dad and me; he was my protector and he would do everything in his power to make sure I was always safe. A special bond, more friends or mates, than father and son.

We arrived at our local GP, I am not entirely sure Dad had

completely grasped of how severe this attack was. When the doctor removed the tea towels and revealed the bloody mess of what was once my calf, now a mangled mess of pink flesh and muscle sinew, he was repulsed and said 'This dog needs to be shot.' The doctor stitched the bottom of the wound to hold the calf to the leg, a temporary patch up, until I could get into surgery. A call was made to Doctor Graeme Southwick, a specialist plastic surgeon and I was raced to Cabrini Malvern, then transferred onto the Avenue in Windsor. Doctor Southwick walked into the room with an air of cool grace, 'I am Doctor Southwick the best plastic surgeon in the country and I will be operating on your leg' and just like that he took control of what turned out to be a disastrous afternoon for all concerned. Poor old Jerusalem Joe must have felt terrible.

Not long after that, we sued the pants off the owners of the dog and received a tidy little pay day for myself when I turned eighteen. For the record the dog was not put down, the law at the time was a dog had to bite three times and I was the dog's second victim. Blood and guts no longer held any fears for me, once you have experienced something like that, you get a new perspective on life.

VICTORIA PARK INTIATION

'There was something about the place...Everyone, from the players to the supporters, walked taller there, felt more confident and brash there.'
— Peter Daicos

The first time I went to Vic Park was 1991. It was a cold, overcast, winter's day and from the moment I stepped into the black and white sarcophagus, there was an overwhelming smell of beer and urine steaming from the old fashioned piss troughs, I just loved the joint.

I was just ten years old but I can recall the day like it was yesterday. My old man had lined up some tickets with a Greek bloke at his work. The deal was we were sitting next to the Sherrin Stand, in the old fashioned boxes with Peter Daicos' parents. Daics is, and always will be, my hero, so you can imagine what this meant to me. The old fashioned boxes consisted of a veneer chipboard partition with a door on hinges and a latch to lock it. Ridiculous, because it didn't separate you from anything, the box only went up to chest height. But any Collingwood supporter reading this will laugh and know exactly what I am talking about. The Greek let us down, my little heart was broken. I had prepared an autograph book and was severely disappointed when Dad broke the news to me. Mum pulled him aside and told him in no uncertain terms, 'You better take this kid to the footy, now Chris.'

So off we went, caught the Frankie line into the city, which was exciting enough. Then we changed platforms to catch the connecting train out to Victoria Park station. Now for any opposition supporter brave enough to come out to the cauldron to face the Pies on our home ground, you have my upmost respect. No words can describe the hostility. To give you an example, some years later I was chatting with a heavily tattooed English bloke out the front of the G while having a smoke. I asked him how he ended up following the Pies, he told me that he happened to go to Vic Park by chance and when he heard the noise and hatred of the opposition by Collingwood people, he said it was the closest thing to the soccer crowds back home and he fell in love.

When you walked down the platform and made a sharp left near the petrol station, there was a guy cooking hot snags, bread and sauce on a barbie. The smell hit you when you got off the train. Dad grabbed me one of them, then he grabbed me a record, sixty cents back then, we entered from the old gates at the corner of Lulie St and Turner St and headed to the other end, where all the ferals would stand and get blind drunk.

As we made our way to the other end, under the stand the noise reverberated around the ground. It was like nothing I had ever heard. The swearing alone was sensational. Dad was always strict with the colourful stuff when I was young. I had no idea you could string so many swear words together. Matt Preston, from *MasterChef*, who is a full blown Collingwood tragic recalls being taken to the chandelier bar at Vic Park. The chandelier bar consisted of a fluoro light under the stand. It was just chaos, the overpowering smell of beer and fast food, the game hadn't even started.

We took our position behind the goals. Dad pushed me up to

the fence with all the other kids so he could watch me, I nestled in behind the point post with my record and waited for the Pies to run out.

As I looked around at the people through a haze of cigarette smoke, barely able to see over the fence, I could not help but feel I belonged to something special. All the supporters were tense and anxious with excitement, smashing down beers and waiting for the mighty Magpies to run out onto the hallowed turf. As they ran out the noise level intensified. Opposition players within earshot of the boundary were bombarded with insults about their mothers' carnal activities. Can you imagine a ten-year-old listening to this? I fronted up at primary school on Monday with my newfound vocabulary, I had my peers eating out of my hand. People would say to me you have the gift of the gab James. Wrong, wrong. I was in the outer at Vic Park when I was ten years old, you cut your teeth there and you can survive anywhere. It must have been an amazing feeling to be a Collingwood player running onto Vic Park. That day we were playing Richmond, our arch enemy from just down the road.

The game was a real shoot out. Daicos up one end going berserk and Jeff Hogg for Richmond up the other doing the exactly the same. This is when footy was pure; no taggers, no tactics, just see ball, get ball. Kick it long to a contest, put your head over the ball and, for fuck's sake, keep your wits about you. Players were always splitting each other down the middle. This was a time when the hip and shoulder was considered a skill. I remember one passage of play in front of the Bob Rose stand. The Richmond defenders had Daicos hemmed in on the boundary and went to push him over. As they did he held out the ball with one hand, dropped it onto his boot and dribbled it through for a goal, his sixth for the day, from memory. The Collingwood faithfuls went off tap, the maestro in front of the social club went bang. I looked around and everyone was high fiving and hugging, I'm pretty sure I probably tried to high five someone, it was just exhilarating for a young bloke. Gee, Daicos was an out and out champion and he loved to play Richmond.

We ended up winning comfortably and there were joyous scenes as we all sung *Good Old Collingwood Forever*. Dad was rapt, he wasn't a drinker but that didn't matter. He used to get that merry after a big win, he may as well have been blind. The walk back to the station with the Collingwood faithful was always entertaining—grown men pissed, playing kick to kick and jumping on each other trying to take speccies. The overall vibe was extremely upbeat.

As we headed towards the city, we approached a station and that is when the fun really started. One pissed Richmond supporter had enough of the jubilant scenes and, against his better judgement, thought he would let the Collingwood-packed train know what he thought of them. The sneaky prick got off and waited till the doors looked, and I repeat, looked like they were about to close. Then he leaned into the carriage from the platform, popped his head in and yelled 'All Collingwood supporters are fucked.' An utterly imbecilic act by a desperate man. To this day I'm not entirely sure what he was hoping to achieve. Dad and I were close to the action. What I remember is seeing a hand shoot from inside the train to grab this Richmond moron by the scruff of the neck, dragging him back into the carriage. It was on. Dad managed to shield me from the altercation, but I still got to see this bloke get a fair old trimming. I was very young but I do remember seeing blood on the wall of the train. Jesus, he got a flogging. After this all calmed down, they dragged him off the train like the disgrace that he was. Dad tried to be diplomatic about not drinking too much and sending a message that violence isn't the answer. 'Fuck that', I thought, from that day on Collingwood and me have been inseparable. Through good times and bad, my love for the Magpies has never wavered. What a great day.

And for the record I have met the great man Peter Daicos. He is one of the most beautiful blokes you will ever met, really humble and understated. Just a lovely human being.

THE RUNNER

'It's supposed to be hard... hard is what makes it great.'
— Jimmy Dugan from A League of Their Own

As a young bloke I couldn't win a sports event to save myself. At primary school sports I was the kid that used to take home the participation award without fail. I was the Hawthorn of participation awards back to back to back. Fuck me it used to give me the shits, because in my mind I really fancied myself as a Usain Bolt type operator.

In grade three, I decided to do something about it. I engaged my father, who was a keen runner, and explained to him that he was to take me running with him. I explained that there was a school running race coming up and I was tired of losing. He must have admired my ambition because we started training straight away.

He was running regularly at the time and decent distances by memory, so at the start he would just ease me into it, by taking on a casual 3km run at slow pace. Here I was running next to him feeling like Robert De Castella. I've always been like that—anytime I take on a task or a goal, I always think I'm the best out there. Positive visualisation; I did that even at a young age, still do. A long time before spirituality, hacky sacks and kale smoothies hit Brunswick Street.

As we got closer to the race, Dad really ramped it up. Towards the end I remember him telling me the runs we were doing for training were the same distances he would run by himself. It was an incredible feeling; training for something and putting in the hard yards. After the run we would cool down in the backyard and I would talk to him about the race. Dad would emphasise the importance of lifting my legs up high and using my arms to generate a good stride and pace. I explained that this kid Jacob was my only real competition, but I was sure he wasn't running big distances, putting kilometres into his legs in preparation. Probably sitting on the couch watching cartoons and stuffing his face with lollies. I was so competitive. This sort of mindset, hating the enemy was something I had most of my life. If you weren't with me, then fuck you. This lolly eating couch potato didn't stand a chance. I was going to tear him apart.

When it came to the big race day, I was nervous. I remember going to the toilet a lot, a trait I inherited from Dad. I had done all the training and all the work, I was completely prepared but I was still nervous as hell.

As we lined up on the blocks, I looked down the line at the competition. Jacob was looking straight ahead, it's go time. *Bang* the gun went and I was off, I knew right from the start that I had everyone covered in that field. It was an incredible feeling; I was out to an early lead. I had a nice little buffer on Jacob, even to this day I can still feel that feeling of flying like Linford Christie across the couch grass. As we approached the halfway mark, I wanted to make sure of my victory so I started to zigzag, cutting off any other runner who might have been a threat. Again I have always had a win-at-all-costs mentality, if I have to cheat to win, then so be it.

As I crossed the finish line first I was flying, it felt like a blur, I was moving that fast. I felt incredible. the teacher came over with the winner's ribbon and I thought, wow, I have actually done it. I looked in the crowd for the old man so I could rejoice in victory with the bloke that got me there, my trainer. He came over and he had a tear in his eye. Looking back, I'm pretty sure he was crying from laughter because I had cut all of the other runners out of the race. It was a special moment in my life.

I learned a valuable lesson. If you want to achieve something worthwhile, no one is going to give it to you—you need to earn that shit.

YOUNG ENTREPRENEUR LAWNS/LOLLIES

'My best entrepreneurial advice is to start.'
— Dave Morin

Making money has always been a passion of mine. I am a bit of journeyman. I'm not afraid to try something new. Ever since I was boy I always had some sort of small business going. I had employees from as early as ten years old. My first business was a car wash; I would wash our cars and then head next door and wash their cars. Showing incredible foresight and business nous, my enthusiasm for the art of the deal became evident when the next-door neighbours' kids wanted to be involved as well. They were too young to know anything about payment, but old enough to help out. So I gave them cloths and buckets and got them doing the heavy lifting, so to speak. I became a director of car washing and finances.

At the end of the wash I would get the neighbour to hand over the money, thank the boys for their help and choof off home. 100 per cent profit and another happy client.

Then there was the lawn mowing round. I would fill up the

lawn mower and whipper snipper with petrol, grab the rake and broom, lay all the equipment across the lawn mower and walk around the local area, cold calling potential customers, setting up a nice little round. I especially targeted overgrown nature strips. It is hard for the occupants to say no to a young kid ready to go with all his gear and your garden is a shambles. I employed a few friends to help but the profits shrunk too much for my liking. So my little brother was engaged to help me out.

Next was my first real crack at employment. It was five days a week and a Saturday morning at the local chemist. This round was a truly prized position and one I had to wait some time to get. I did the bulk of the days, my sister did another day or two and I sub-contracted Carlos to do the big days I didn't want to do.

The job involved riding my bike with a backpack and delivering tablets and medicine to elderly people who couldn't leave their houses. I was drug dealing even back then. It was a prick of a job when it rained, so occasionally Mum would drive us in the car. When I initially took the job on, I did it every day to get a feel for it and I learned what days I would get the best customers, meaning the ones that would give generous tips. Mr Edbrooke was a beauty, smoking his Camel cigarettes, he would put his hand in a loose change bowl and give whatever he scooped up. One day I received about $14 which was a fortune then. Another notable tipper was the big rock spider that lived on McKinnon Rd. He would regularly tip $5 and really enjoyed it when the kids dropped off his supplies. He would come to the front door salivating, overwhelmed by the younger company. We were all warned about him; you had to stay on your toes at his place.

Then there was the confectionery wholesaler next to Malvern station. I made up an order list of all the different bits and pieces: sherbets, pineapples, snakes, violet crumbles, raspberries, all of the favourites. Then off I would go around the neighbourhood taking orders and cash. I would tally up my orders and head to the wholesaler to buy sweets in bulk. When I got home I would break them into smaller bundles, repackage and on-sell it. This was quite a good business, the feedback was very encouraging and it appealed to the customer's weakness: sugar, door-to-door sugar. My customers would go inside with their loot and disguise their addictions by saying, 'Oh I'm just supporting the young kid having a go, great to see a young fella with that drive.' Make no mistake about the choice of product on my part, I knew exactly what I was doing.

It was this last business that really opened my eyes. It was interesting to see how easy it is to sell your product to an addict. They loved it and would eagerly await your return.

SHINER... DAMIAN AND RIKKI STORY

'Nobody can give you freedom. Nobody can give you equality or justice or anything. If you're a man, you take it.'
— Malcolm X

I copped a lot of shit for only starting puberty in year nine. I was a late developer. My legs didn't really have any hair on them and for that, a few of the guys suggested I was most likely a little light on hair in the pubic region as well. Damian was the ring leader; a skinny Italian kid with two older brothers. Damian was a talented footballer and most likely would have been drafted, had he not been vertically challenged. He was an interesting looking individual. He had an abnormally large forehead that was really long and on the right side of this forehead he had this lump. To match the lump Damian had a massive nose. His side profile looked the Himalayas, but I let all of this go, I didn't mention it ... until much later.

Damian the Lump and a couple of guys started calling me Shiner. Boys being boys all joined in and it wasn't long before this shit got out of hand. I wasn't used to being on the receiving end of this sort of foul slander and the Lump was really enjoying himself.

One day we were in the gymnasium watching the seniors play basketball. This was always fun because we got out of class and basketball is a game that I have always loved. The Lump decided it would be a good idea to get the rest of the class to start singing 'C'mon on baby wax my shiner' to the tune of the Doors song, *Light My Fire,* which, to his credit, was pretty funny. Even back then I could appreciate the humour in it, but after months of this shiner business, it had worn thin and I had had enough.

I walked to where the toughest kid in the school was sitting and the Lump and the rest of his choir immediately fell silent. My plan had already succeeded without me taking any action. I approached Rikki, the tough guy, and asked him if one bottle of bourbon was a fair payment to wait at Malvern Station and open a can of whoop-ass on the Lump. As I said this I looked over and pointed in his general direction. Rikki nodded. I told Rikki to leave it with me and I would organise payment, time and date. This was my first involvement in organised crime and I have to say it was very productive.

As I sat back down in my chair the silence was deafening, None of the choir knew who I had put in the gun. The Lump definitely knew he was in the gun and looked like Coyote from the Roadrunner cartoon as he is about to fall off a cliff. As luck would have it, one of Rikki's good mates was sitting next to the Lump. I didn't quite catch what the Lump asked him but Rikki's mate said 'Lump, you are going to get your arse kicked, Rikki doesn't fuck around.' With that I sat back and let fear do the work for me. Job done. Fear is an incredible tool if it's used properly. It's easy to work out that fear is more effective than actual violence. The anticipation and threat of pain can send someone into the dark corridors of self-doubt and the Lump was well and truly down that long and lonely hallway. He was all by himself, the bravado and courage had evaporated, he was now struggling to swallow and maintain his composure. His need to gain acceptance from his peers had failed. No one wanted to know him now, out of the fear of getting hurt themselves. I let the uncertainty marinate for a few days, he didn't know when it was coming or how. It was fascinating to watch the Lump get around like a dog walking on polished floor boards with socks on.

The funny thing is, I didn't even want to hurt the Lump and I never followed through with the order. But a precedent had been set and no one bothered me much after that, which was a feat in itself as I was a real smart-ass. Later, the Lump and I became close, we actually spent quite a bit of time together. He had a lovely family and his older brothers were hilarious. But the Lump always felt the need to be sarcastic and give people shit. He really struggled with women and if it wasn't for yours truly setting him up with a girl that I can only describe as 'wild', he would still be a virgin at twenty. Lump was just an insecure kid finding his way in life by projecting negative attention away from himself and towards other people.

DOGGY STYLE AND THE COIN TOSS

'There is no such thing as good money and bad money. There's just money.'
— Lucky Luciano

After my first taste with organised crime, after having successfully planted the seed of fear in Lump, I have to say it really grew on me. The power was addictive and the thrill of having control over someone else was exciting. My main focus was myself and making sure I was treated with the respect I felt that I deserved. But every now and again someone comes along to test you and it's pretty obvious that you need to eliminate the problem.

For business management class we had to set up a small business at school and work out our profit/loss, outgoings and everything associated with running a business. The thought of this was tantalising for me, making money has never been a problem. I teamed up with another couple of guys and we decided to run a hot dog stand and call it 'Doggy Style'. It was a great idea and would have worked but the teachers canned it, on the account of the name. I would not budge. It was the central focus of the business and its main drawcard. The teacher, to his credit, laughed and liked the name, but being a Catholic school run by brothers, it was never going to fly. So to stick it right up the school and the brothers, I organised a huge piece of laminated chipboard with different amounts of money penned in little squares: 50 cents, $3, $5, $10 and so on. The highest being $20 and if you landed a coin in the certain section of the $20 square, it was $20 x 2 = $40, a lot of money for a school kid, but also a massive incentive.

All you needed were gold coins to play and you would toss the coin and try and land it inside the square to get that amount of money. This was my first foray into illegal gambling, it was always going to be a success. The idea of the task was to gain business management experience.

It took off like wild fire, the kids queued up, three deep to take their chance at winning some cold, hard cash. There were even teachers coming over to have a shot and look at the commotion. I was directing the play, there was a bag man collecting the money, a guy scooping the losing bets off the table and three guys giving change and making sure it was all sweet.

By lunchtime the business management teacher came over and said the people running the canteen had complained because their takings were way down. I asked him if I was going to get a high distinction, instead he told me to wrap it up after lunch because it was out of control; I was amazed at how the kids would rather gamble their money, instead of buying food. Money was flying in and I loved every minute of it. I upped the ante and doubled everything on the table for the last ten minutes. 'That's right guys any prize is paying double,' I yelled. The crowd went mad; people were screaming and pushing each other to get their bets on.

Then out of nowhere this little fucker, who had a head like the guy on *Mad Magazine*, landed his coin on the 2 x $20. That had been doubled, so he was due to collect $80. What I did was look at where the coin had landed, it was good but I quickly moved it, so no one got the chance to see it. But this little prick was adamant he had landed a good toss. Now he was yelling—or trying to yell, his voice was breaking and he was making a terrible noise. He yelled, 'I want my money back,' over and over again and he got louder. I grabbed two of my boys and told them to take him over near the bushes and out of the way a bit, just hang back. The *Mad Magazine* kid was bad for business, so with him out of the way the punters kept punting.

I marched over there and grabbed him by his shirt and dragged him out of sight, then I told him in my most threatening voice, 'I'll give you $5 and that's it, if you continue with this shit you won't get a cent and I'll punch the fuck out of you. Your choice.'

He took the money and left. The key to the lesson I learned was that the threat of violence and a little bit of cash is very effective when it comes to negotiation. Gambling is an amazing way to make fast money. I have never seen anything like that day and it was only a coin toss board, imagine a casino. With a business that involves cash money and illegality you have to be ready and willing to go to extreme lengths to get what you want. But the most important lesson: be quick on your feet and even quicker to act.

LOST INNOCENCE

'Scar tissue is stronger than regular tissue. Realize the strength, move on.'
—Henry Rollins

Carlos and I were sixteen and the song on the radio that summer was 'Breakfast At Tiffany's' by Deep Blue Something. We were all off to a house party in Ormond and it was the night that would change our lives forever. Carlos, who was always working at the local pizza shop, managed to swing a night off. The party was set to be huge. I had my tall, blonde, leggy missus there—she was a bit of a show-stopper, even at that age. The Flower (my missus) had a lot of Maria Sharapova about her and tonight she was wearing this short, black, skin-tight, Quicksilver dress and white sandals. She was the original surfer chick.

As we walked to the party from my place I had the feeling that it was going be a special night. When we arrived at this beautiful two-storey period home, our gang Ramey, Duey, Carlos, Tiles, Ripley, the Flower and myself, said hello to everyone and settled in for a good night. We knew everyone there as we were friendly kids that didn't look for trouble. I never used to drink, which gave me the opportunity to observe with a clear mind. Carlos and the Fainter were getting stuck right into it. Carlos' dad would drink to oblivion, so it was no surprise that Carlos was doing the same. He was paralytic in a short space of time and was hugging me and telling me how much he loved me. I used to get around and talk to as many people as I could. Being a teetotaller was fun because you got to see how the drink would make certain people happy or sad or aggressive. It didn't bother me; I enjoyed talking to people and connecting. What I did find interesting was when people got drunk they found it easier to be honest and real with their emotions. So even though I wasn't drinking, it was the honesty and vulnerability that I enjoyed sharing with people at the party. Once I had connected with someone, I would eventually find myself talking to other people. As the evening wore on and the alcohol began to flow, so did the hugs and kisses. It was pretty cool.

I guess you could say I was reasonably tuned in to people's moods and I had a good understanding of how to read a situation. My intuition has always been a great strength of mine and, as luck would have it, I could sense things happening. That night seemed no different but there was a sinister feeling I couldn't put my finger on.

The Flower's dad picked her up from my place at 11pm, so we would walk home at about 10 to give myself plenty of time to work my night moves. We would both get into my back bungalow and start throwing shapes. Then, sure enough, at 11pm you could hear the rumble of the vintage V8 Statesman her dad had; what a beautiful car the old Statesman was. After the Flower left I went back into my bungalow and lay on my bed for a little while, contemplating calling it a night. Something I felt deep inside called me to get up and go back to that party, so I did.

When I arrived back, I noticed it was in full swing—there was a new bunch of guys there, guys I had never met before. There was one particular bloke, an older guy who was really agitated, Charlie.

Being the outgoing type, I made my way over to introduce

myself and gauge his temperament. Charlie was a lean, Arabic-looking bloke with light eyes and an unsettled vibe about him. He had a Lebanese cedar tree earring in one ear. Charlie told me that no one would let him play his song on the juke box and it had upset him. Some other guys I knew, blokes that you would call young hoods, were making it clear to Charlie that his presence wasn't wanted. There was definitely going to be a fight if Charlie stayed, so he did the smart thing and went home. Little did anyone know how seriously Charlie took his song playing and selection at the juke box. We were about to find out. As he left I crossed him in the hallway and asked him why he was going, he said 'Yeah those guys are being racist and won't let me play my song', so we said goodnight and left it at that.

Timing is an incredible thing: a couple of seconds here or there can make a lifetime of difference. Carlos and the Fainter were steaming drunk and completely unaware of what they were doing, so I slowly started rounding them up to take them home. I could have easily just walked home by myself, picked up some Maccas and been home within half an hour. But big Carlos felt compelled to say goodnight to every single person at the party, including people he had never met before.

We were all now out the front and rejoicing at what a great evening it was. Carlos rarely got out so he was enjoying the last moments of a night on the town. At last we managed to break free from the throng and walk down Park St towards McDonald's. Part of me was thinking, 'Okay we are on the home stretch here we can just relax and enjoy the drunk talk', which was always one of my favourite parts of going to a local house party. Another part of me was still very much aware that there was still a bit left in the evening.

Three-quarters of the way down the street towards Maccas is where it all went down. I was just a little bit ahead on my skateboard when I turned around to see an old, greenish Celica right behind Carlos and the Fainter. Much to my shock that car drove over the top of Carlos. All of a sudden, Carlos screamed, 'Hey Cassa! It's me Carlos, it's Carlos.' Poor Carlos was so pissed he didn't realise he was in danger. He thought it was one of our mates Cassa. It was clear to me then and there that this situation was about to get real. I picked up the skateboard as a weapon and prepared myself for what was about to take place.

Both the passenger and the driver doors opened and the assailants stepped out of the car. It was dark and even though the lights were shining brightly from the car, they were shining towards us. I couldn't see that one of them had a large pruning saw and the other had a blunt object. One of the assailants charged towards me and the other towards Carlos. I held the skateboard like I was about to swing it and started walking backwards quickly. So quickly I launched backwards over a brick fence and lay there.

As I lay in the garden bed, what came out of Carlos are noises that I can never forget. Cries and screams of pain and innocence were lost as Carlos rolled around drunk on the road while the two armed maniacs attacked him. The sound of metal grating against the road, when the man with the pruning saw slashed at my sixteen-year-old friend. Carlos screamed and, as much as I wanted to be the hero, jump over the fence and attack these men with my skateboard, I couldn't. I was frozen and I was terrified, the feeling was indescribable—that feeling of fear and not being able to be there for my best mate, who was now lying on the road of Park St in Ormond. It became a scar that I would carry for a long time, the scar of a coward. To me, it didn't matter that it was over so quickly, I would not have been able to do much even if I had become involved. The shame I carried of being too scared for my own safety is a shame that was compounded when I finally did get up and see Carlos walking towards me with blood oozing out of two open wounds. All I could see of him was the whites of his eyes. There was blood everywhere.

Some people said if Carlos hadn't been drunk this may not have happened, we may not have taken so long to leave the party. What I heard later at the hospital was if he hadn't been so drunk, Carlos may not have been able to handle the enormity of the situation.

There was a wound the size and length of an adult ring finger just above his temple and a deep wound the size and length of an adult middle finger just above his jaw bone. The people who did this were serious about causing harm. He looked at me as he staggered towards me, his eyes said help. Blood was gushing out of the wound above his jaw bone.

The Fainter emerged from wherever he was and, surprisingly, Carlos wanted to head back to the party. Carlos and I both knew we couldn't go to his parents' house—his dad would have killed us.

When we arrived back at the party it was mayhem. I can safely say no one there had been around or involved in an ultra-violent incident before. The women and girls out the front of the party started hyperventilating and having panic attacks, the blokes were just staring, no one knew what to do or say. It was time to take control of this. I grabbed Carlos who had staggered up onto the front porch and I yelled at the Fainter who kept fainting and falling over. I grabbed them both and got them moving down the street. I started talking to Carlos and kept talking to him and encouraging him, 'It's gonna be alright mate, we will go back to my place and we will get some bandages, Dad used to work at Smith and Nephew, so we have heaps of gauze and stuff to sort it out.' Carlos was actually in really good spirits, which helped the situation. He told me I could have his dog if he died and the Fainter could have his computer. In no time, we were half way home.

The blood had started to congeal on his skin. On the corner of Murray Rd and Cadby Ave Carlos asked me if it was bad and when he asked this question, he put his tongue through the wound in his cheek and touched it with his finger. You never forget things like that. I didn't answer, we just kept moving. Soon we arrived at my place and I laid Carlos on the back lawn and the Fainter, well, true to form, he fainted next to him. I ran into my parents' room and told then there had been an incident.

Mum and Dad were fantastic. Dad dressed his wounds and mum undressed him. We gave him some of my old clothes and mum washed what he was wearing. I remember this because she said the water turned red in the washing machine. Dad made the dreaded call to Carlos' older brother, the Smoker, and explained what had happened. The Smoker was there within minutes. When he saw the state of his younger brother, who was bandaged and in much better shape than he was before, the Smoker just shook his head in disgust. I felt some of that disgust directed at me.

The trip to Monash hospital was a silent one. Carlos was sitting in the front seat with a bucket, the shock had now worn off and he was feeling drowsy. When he was admitted, Carlos managed to sneak off to the toilet where he passed out and smashed his head on the toilet bowl, he was found concussed. Carlos was operated on and had plastic surgery for numerous stitches on both wounds and there were many more superficial wounds on his forearms and body, where he had managed to defend himself. I slept in the Smoker's car downstairs in the emergency carpark.

It turned out the music lover from the party, Charlie, had gone home and got his father and headed back to the party for revenge. Instead of going into the party and directing their revenge on the appropriate people, they just drove down the street and attacked some innocent kids. Now I would happily put up my hand and admit if we had done the wrong thing. But let me tell you, they should have known better. Both father and son did some minor jail time for grievous bodily harm.

This was the moment our lives changed forever. We lost our innocence in Park St, Ormond that night. The innocence of youth was torn out of our hearts by a revenge-stricken adolescent and his father, all over a song on a juke box. Carlos and I became suspicious of people, less trusting. We began to think everyone had an angle and was trying to harm us. It is awful to think that way and it took me years to understand the significance of the experience. Then even longer again to gain closure on the guilt I carried with me. I internalised the situation and made it my fault. After that I felt responsible for Carlos' scars and for Carlos going forward.

The positive was that we became blood brothers over our dance with the devil and for years we became a team that was unbreakable. This was only the beginning of a wild ride; Carlos and I were like two bandits with the pedal to the metal.

Not long after this we both started experimenting with acid, which to me now was a good indicator of the effect this incident had on both of us. We longed to escape. The truth was we felt as though we had both been let down and violated by society. We were young and didn't understand how to deal with our emotions, so we began to self-medicate. Acid was our first port of call. Most kids experiment with smoking and the drinking, not us, we went straight into the mind-altering world of LSD.

I have heard if you take more than ten acid trips in your lifetime you can be considered legally insane, acid never leaves your body like other drugs and this is why you have flashbacks. I once took ten tabs in two hours, there is no other drug like acid in my opinion, but it's not for everyone. There are certain people who completely lose the plot if they dropped one. Carlos and I had lived a nightmare; we weren't really scared of anything from there on in.

FROM NO.1 IN AUSTRALIA TO APPRENTICE WAGES

'People don't buy for logical reasons. They buy for emotional reasons.'
— Zig Ziglar

Not long after I had come back from schoolies, the question of employment reared its ugly head. Mum was working with a woman and this woman had a friend, the Patroller. The Patroller was a manager/director at a company that was selling Optus. Optus was a relatively new player in the telecommunication scene in Australia. It had been under the Telecom/Telstra regime for some time. They had control of the market and the prices, so Optus was set to give it a good shake up. They were offering 20 cents local phone calls instead of Telstra's 25 cents, a new handset, cheaper line rental, no handset rental and so on. It was a real no brainer and as a rule people were fed up with not having another option, they were happy to try something new.

We were given allocations that consisted of thirty houses or addresses every night and we would knock on their doors and convince them to come over to Optus. The day started when we arrived at the head office in Lonsdale St in the city at around 12pm and headed out to the area we were targeting at around 2pm, then we would work those addresses until 8 or 9pm. People arrived home from work at around five, so we would be hovering around at exactly that time.

The Patroller gave me a fifteen-minute job interview and I was offered a position as a sales rep. At this stage you had to be eighteen to cold call. Being seventeen, well, we all just pretended like that didn't matter. Good country. We received two weeks training and then we were out in the suburbs selling, door-to-door. The Patroller put me with two of the best salesmen in the company for my first week. This happened to be a stroke of genius. I was like a sponge learning from these guys and their techniques. Manipulating body language, reading people's mannerisms; the art of reading between the lines and trusting your intuition. They were extremely talented at persuasion and influencing. I would check my fingers after shaking their hands. Very slick operators indeed. It was a case of swimming with sharks and these sharks were teaching me how to bite. These sharks were grown men, some of them with families. I was a young, impressionable kid learning the secrets of closing deals and getting people to do what you want. I just happened to be in the right place, at the right time.

The pay structure was a free phone and a $300 retainer every week. You needed to make thirty sales in a week to receive full commission, that was six sales a night. One sale equated to $35 in your pocket and if you convinced the same customer to purchase Optus Vision as well, the deal was worth $60. The record for the week when I started was around fifty and the best anyone sold for an evening was around ten to twelve.

My second night out there I sold thirteen and on my best week: ninety-two. I broke every company record within the first month.

The whole sales thing came naturally to me. A lot of sales people wore suits and ties but my style was nice jeans and a Ralph Lauren polo. My whole approach was very relaxed. Sometimes I would approach a house right on dinner time and end up eating dinner with the family, while closing the deal. One Saturday afternoon I closed twenty-one deals, hungover like a dog. I had come straight from Frostbites in Chapel St.

Another Saturday in Newport, someone showed me there was a long distance phone carrier that you could access through the Optus network with 19 cent-per-minute phone calls to Lebanon. This was 1998, mind you, things hadn't progressed to the level of technology we have now. A long distance phone call was the only way to communicate with your relos and let's face it, Lebanese people are all about family. It was highly illegal to be telling people about that sort of cheat, but hey, I was very much about doing illegal things. When I explained to the first Lebanese family how it worked with the 19 cent-per-minute phone call back home; that family rang another family on the spot, then another family and another family. Newport was turned on its head that day and I reaped the rewards. It could have gone on well into Saturday night, but the Station Hotel in Greville St was calling. I can't remember exactly how many deals I did that day, but it was huge. There was a massive cash bonus waiting for me back at the office. One day when I got home from work, Mum had printed an email from her work colleague to leave on the table. It read: 'Your son, James, is the number one sales representative in Australia.' I was seventeen.

The company that employed me was not entirely above board, but that suited my style. If you have seen *The Wolf of Wall Street* or *Boiler Room* that would give you a better idea of what I was dealing with. It didn't bother me in the slightest, the money was still green and was coming in hot. As a seventeen-year-old kid in 1998, I was clearing anywhere from $1200 to $2000 plus cash bonuses on a Saturday arvo for the superstars.

All this cash was great because when it came to living large and spending big, I was right up there with the best. Dad lost the plot one day when I purchased a pair of $600 Dolce and Gabbana boots, 'who the fuck do you think you are, Kerry Packer?' For the record, I gave them to the Salvation Army this year, they were still fine. $600 for nineteen years of use, not bad really.

There was little he could do; my fat pay cheques coincided with a massive cash injection from when we sued the people for the dog attack. Tiles, my Italian mate from primary school, had an uncle down at the docks that landed him a pretty sweet job doing night shift unloading containers and he was earning some pretty fat cash himself. The two of us were real men about town, living it up at the casino, buying expensive clothes and partying with women. Great times but times like these are never meant to last.

My Nanna, God love her, had been diagnosed with breast cancer. She had been fighting it for a while and was doing okay. But it was family drama that finally tipped her over the edge. This stress was the straw that broke the camel's back. She never fully recovered, it was a devastating blow.

Altona Meadows, was the area I was working in when Dad called me in tears from Nannas' house. Dad didn't really cry unless it was serious. He told me that I'd better come quick, 'Son, Nanna has taken a turn for the worse.' I told the team leader and called a cab. When I got to Nanna's house there were people everywhere. Mum found me and took me into her room. Nanna was lying on her bed. Mum pushed me closer to her and said 'Go and talk to her, talk in her ear, she can hear you.' As I got closer to Nanna's body I could feel that she was in the process of passing over. She was cold and a lot of the life had already left her face. Then I grabbed her hand and leaned in to her ear and said 'It's James, Nanna, I love you.' She didn't move much or say anything but in my heart that wasn't important. She knew that I was with her at the end. We all stayed there till it was late, but apparently later that evening when we left,

Nanna threw her arms up in the air. It would have been amazing to know what made her do that. The angels in heaven where waiting with open arms for that woman, I do know that much.

She passed away that night; Dad came into my back bungalow and told me. One of the saddest things I have ever seen was my brother's reaction the next morning when my parents told him. He was very close with both my grandparents and the poor little bugger just burst into tears, it broke my heart to see him like that, he adored Nanna, they were so close.

The funeral was massive. It turns out Nanna had touched quite a few people. Most of Bentleigh rolled out to send her off in a fitting tribute.

After the funeral, I didn't have the tools to cope with the loss but drinking seemed to numb the pain. Being a salesman no longer held much interest for me, my passion was gone. The company gave me some time off and were fantastic about it. When I came back it was to no avail, you need the killer instinct to be good at sales and my teeth and claws had become blunt. It petered out into nothing and I left Optus with no real prospects, a drinking problem and 10kg overweight.

All that money was no good for me, I became self-centred and out of touch with who I was. Money is a great leveller. If you don't know what you're doing it can take you to lofty heights and drop you just as quickly. I didn't like the person I had become.

My godfather, Sven, asked me to come to one of his building sites and help out. It was very kind of him to get me out of the house and working again, my confidence was shot and I felt washed up at nineteen. The maniac used to flog his employees so I gained strength and fitness. With that came self-worth and, a tan from working outside. The next thing I knew I was flying again. I associated feeling good with the job. Carpentry has never been something I have enjoyed, my decision to take up a carpentry apprenticeship that I didn't really love, was another valuable lesson.

I was paid $160 a week as a first year apprentice carpenter, even now that is hard to say. I resorted to arm wrestling blokes in pubs for extra spending money. I did it though, driving out to Kensington every day and slugging it out with a bloke named Darryl. My heart was never in it and I have no doubt it was evident in my work ethic. Rather than go to bed early to be fresh for work, Carlos and myself were pulling bongs in parks till all hours. Then I would front up to work the next morning with my eyes as red as the devil's dick. At a guess, one would assume my attitude could be best described as lethargic. For $160 a week, it wasn't really much incentive, not for the number one sales rep in Australia.

So Darryl let me go when he finished all the houses in his development at Kensington and I was glad to see the back of him. The bloke played Triple J and liked the snow. It was surf and Triple M for me all day long. It was only a small thing but as people, we were streets apart.

THE STATION HOTEL FIGHT

'He will win who knows when to fight and when not to fight.'
— Sun Tzu

There was a huge group of us going to the Station Hotel on a Saturday night. This was at around the time that I had just turned eighteen. The hotel employed a quality door guy to make sure the right people got into the place. My older cousins had a connection with this particular door guy and we always got in without any dramas. It was a very enjoyable evening, none of us started any trouble and I ended up kissing two women from an office I had worked in briefly.

I saw these sexy older women at the bar, one with blonde hair and long legs and the other one had brown frizzy hair that really stood out. I decided to kiss the blonde who was drinking champagne. The blonde was taken back initially, but she reciprocated and started giggling. Then I leaned in and kissed the frizzy-haired woman, who kissed me back. My confidence was sky high by this stage, so I asked the two of them to kiss each other and then kiss me. Off they went, pashing each other at the bar. Then they stopped and grabbed me and both kissed me at the same time. I was so overwhelmed with my enormous erection, I didn't bother to look around and see if anyone had seen this. Fuck, it would have looked good.

As the evening started to wrap up, we knew we had a beautiful house in Armadale to go back to and smoke some weed. As we walked out of the hotel, there was a group of blokes looking bored and keen for a fight. We walked straight past them and down Greville Street towards Chapel Street. This drunk bloke came over to me and started annoying me, so I took my shirt off and did the Ali double-shuffle shadow boxing in the middle of the street. Everyone was laughing and having a good time when the drunk lunged forward and tried to shove me, so I grabbed his wrist and used his momentum to throw him head first into the bushes. We all kept walking on but the previous group we passed decided they were keen for a fight and to use this incident to start up with our gang. Now what these eight older blokes didn't see was there was, in fact, fifteen of us. And even though we were inexperienced, we weren't shy by any stretch of the imagination. The other gang let their ambitions get in the way. They were seriously outnumbered.

It was on like Donkey Kong, we were all into it and the fight was under our control right from the start. The only problem I had was that my mate Ramey had just cut his arm with the drop saw and it was still healing—one bloke had targeted him because he had his arm in a plaster cast. Ripley and I punched the living suitcases out of this bloke and I laid the big D+G boots right into his ribcage with the vicious callousness of Robert De Niro in *Goodfellas*. Then Ramey got up and joined in as well.

The fight fanned out into a series of one-on-ones on Greville Street. I went toe-to-toe with another bloke from their party. There is nothing organised about a street fight at all. If you can withstand pain and go for longer, you usually win. There is no feeling like being locked into a stand-up punch on, it's exhilarating and exciting. The fear of getting seriously hurt always had me on edge, not scared, more aware and in the moment. I finished him off and left him lying where I found him.

It was an epic blue. Ripley was thrown through a shop-front window and grabbed a pair of boots for himself while he was in the shop. It spilled out onto Chapel Street right near the Court Jester. I was letting roundhouse kicks go right in the middle of Chapel Street with traffic going either side of us. We all split up and knew to meet up back at the Fainter's joint in Armadale.

When we all got back there it was insane, the testosterone and energy in the room, blokes came in screaming, 'How fucked was that?' Blokes were hugging and retelling their version of events. One bloke commented that he didn't realise we were such mad cunts, he wanted to come out with us more. It was such an enjoyable evening, we all lit up some joints and listened to music.

WEAK AS PISS SON

'All that lives must die, passing through nature to eternity.'
— William Shakespeare

After Nanna passed away, Gramps was never the same. I knew this because Mum used to make extra dinner for him and I used to drive it round there while it was still hot. Gramps permanently had a tear in his eye since the love of his life passed away. He had set up a shrine of photos with Nanna and himself around his dinner table. So they all faced him when he ate and read the papers. It was a little bit of self-therapy to help ease the pain.

I decided to organise a tribute of my own so I had a tattoo done on my forearm with 'Nanna' on it. When I showed Gramps he was very impressed. Keep in mind, this is when tattoos were still tattoos—you didn't have hipsters with beards getting full sleeves to go with their chai lattes.

Gramps put on a brave face for everyone, but deep down I could sense he was really hurting. He yearned for her company.

Their love started with a pregnancy out of wedlock and blossomed into devotion.

It must be terribly hard when you have been with someone your whole life and then they are gone. The emptiness would have been very unsettling for him.

Gramps started to become unwell and was taken to the hospital. When I went in there to see him I gave him a kiss and asked how he was, he replied, 'Weak as piss, son.' I honestly think he had had enough of life and wanted to be reunited with his soul mate.

At this point, I was beginning to consume drugs on a more regular basis and was hanging around some fairly average types. There was a chop shop round the corner from my parents' house. The bloke running the show was a young bloke called Northy, he was only seventeen but he loved stealing cars. The problem was he didn't have anyone to sell anything to. He just stole high performance Holden cars, chopped them up and left them at his house. He had a little bit of dash, but no brains at all. We'd go to his place and sit on Clubsports car seats, it was ridiculous. Northy was red-hot and it didn't take the police long to start watching him. Once we were over at his place and we saw a camera flash through the window, we all thought we were seeing things. Not long after this police raided his home. The flash was the cop's surveillance team.

I was never going to be around a crew like this too long; it was more of a case of building my network. Even around a pack of jokers like this gang, you may meet someone who was organised.

It was a tough time for the family, with Gramps being sick and me not helping the situation by running with these clowns. Word was filtering back to my parents about what I was up to and they were riding me pretty hard. I didn't care. It was my turn to do exactly as I pleased. Then we got the news we all knew was coming: Gramps had passed away. It was a very emotional time for Mum, she was hurting and was really upset with me. She asked me if

I was going to come to the funeral, which was a fair old whack and probably something I deserved. If she needed me to be her whipping boy, that was okay. I was big enough to handle it.

The funeral was a sad affair. At the wake all the men sat on the front porch and got drunk. What else was there to do? My parents had a go at me for getting drunk too. Our relationship had become unworkable; I wasn't going to stop what I was doing. In fact, I had plans to become a full blown criminal, this was only the beginning. What I needed to do was get away from the family and the area, so I could move around without people reporting everything back to my parents. It was the only way, everything I was doing was upsetting them and I was tired of listening to them castigate me for my behaviour.

Gramps was gone now. It was time for me to move on, there was a big wide world out there and I wanted to go and investigate its deep, dark corners. Nanna and Gramps were the glue that held the family together, without them there was very little appeal. Just a bunch of uppity Sri Lankans bitching about each other.

WHERE THE WILD THINGS ARE

'Learning is always rebellion ... every bit of new truth discovered is revolutionary to what was believed before.'
— Margaret Lee Runbeck

After finishing with Darryl, I pumped weights, ran and worked with Carlos delivering pizza for a summer until my pre-apprenticeship course started in February the next year. During this period, we both began to spend a lot of time with his cousin Chewy. The bloke had grown up in the heart of St. Kilda in the 80s and had a good foothold in Prahran. Chewy was a bit older than us, but experience-wise we were chalk and cheese. He showed us ways to cheat and angles to take to get what you want and to get people to do what you want. He showed us how to intimidate and influence people and, most of all, how to make money ... illegally.

In my eyes, I had tried to do the right thing, do the hard yards and get an apprenticeship. But I was disillusioned by what had happened with Darryl and the dismal pay felt like a slap in the face. So even though I did go on to complete the carpentry pre-apprenticeship and continue my apprenticeship with Sven, my career in the underworld had begun.

Sven was my honorary godfather. He married my cousin and we clicked straight away. Sven is 6'6" with massive hands and a solid appetite for a good time. Sven was from Airport West and he knew how to handle himself. He taught me a lot about business and life. He was a good entertainer and he always let me invite my friends to his parties. He is a great guy and I am lucky to have him in my life as a friend and sounding board for advice.

Here I was already hustling and rock 'n' rolling. Carpentry and building were getting further and further away as I went full steam ahead into a life that was much more exciting and the rewards were a hell of a lot more enjoyable. Everything normal and legal was becoming less and less important, including my family. It was my time to spread my wings. Rules and regulations left me feeling dissatisfied and disenchanted with the universe. So fuck the rules, it was time for me to do exactly as I pleased. Jamesy had been a good boy for long enough.

NO UNIVERSITY FOR GANGSTERS

'Judges, lawyers and politicians have a license to steal. We don't need one.'
— Carlos Gambino

There aren't any courses you can do to become a gangster and there isn't any room for people who want to enter that world with a late start. You are born into that life, the survival instincts and ability to earn are ingrained from an early age. There's the tale of two men: one man had experience and the other man had money, not long after they met, the man with the experience left with the money and the man with the money left with experience.

There are all sorts of people in the industry. Some get called rats because they would do anything to survive, including giving people up. Rats are, not only the lowest form of humans in that world, but also the most dangerous. They can and have brought down multi-million dollar empires just by opening their mouths.

I was always interested in the lifestyle because it was exciting and different. I was ninteen or twenty when Carlos' cousin, Chewy, introduced us to the scene. We both saw an opportunity to learn and gain some experience. Chewy also saw an opportunity, which was to earn off two eager young bucks and work his way back up a ladder on which he once held a nice position.

Chewy's story is good enough to fill another book, but out of respect for him I will keep it brief. Chewy grew up around Chapel Street in St. Kilda when it was still wild. You could not give houses away in St. Kilda in the 80s. Crime was full-on and Chewy grew up in the middle of it. His house was situated where all the sex workers and pimps plied their trade. He was connected to serious people and was involved in some interesting projects. The whole situation went pear-shaped when people he thought were his friends did the wrong thing by him. Not only did he end up owing a lot of money to the serious people, he was facing jail time. Some men came and dragged Chewy out of his house and took him to a meeting in Como Park. These gangsters let a shot go right next to his ear. Chewy said when it happened everything went quiet and he didn't know whether he was dead or alive. I can only imagine how that must have felt, an incident like that takes years off your life.

So Chewy was an angry, distrusting and washed up crook looking to get back on top. He was overweight and not happy with the world, but he had a wealth of experience to draw on and still had a few friends he could call on. Carlos and I teamed up with him and we all used each other to earn money and get ahead. It wasn't a conventional friendship with Chewy, as you will come to understand. But nothing is conventional when you are involved in this world. You have to be flexible and able to adapt if you want to survive.

AND SO IT BEGINS ...

'I'm your huckleberry, that's just my game.'
— Doc Holliday from Tombstone

As fate would have it, I happened to be partial to a conversation at the Marine Hotel in Brighton between a marijuana grower and a marijuana dealer. Not exactly the stomping ground for serious knockabouts, but, hey, who was I to judge? They were both talking about a bloke called Lance who apparently had taken a large consignment of choof but reneged on paying these two characters back. To be brutally honest, I could understand where Lance was coming from—these two, who were bitching so passionately about payment, probably didn't have the physical strength to tear apart a plastic bag. So I decided to inject myself in the conversation with, 'The reason he hasn't paid you blokes is that you're not exactly intimidating, are you?'

The Choof Chariot looked at me with shock and disdain. Despite what their egos were telling them, they both knew I was speaking the truth. I didn't give them an opportunity to think about this at all; my next course of action was to demand Lance's address and all the details I needed to sort this out. I established that Lance lived alone, he was a big unit, he had a large German shepherd that he kept in the backyard and rarely left the house. Lance was also a Brighton operator, which meant he was as weak as piss. The Choof Chariot was clearly impressed by the young bloke with dash and offered me $5000 if I could get Lance to pay them back. They were desperate for an outcome.

At that point, I had no idea how I was going to do this, but I sure as hell wasn't going to tell them that. I grabbed both their licences and kept them for insurance. The Choof Chariot weren't overly pleased with my request, but what the hell were they going to do? Armed with the address and the reward of a $5k purse, I went over to Lance's place for a couple of days and sat off the joint to study his routine. True to form, he didn't go outside very often.

Lance had a stream of people coming and going from his house until late into the night, obviously clients buying choof but never before 11am when this happy hoofer would wake up. Lance would walk his dog around this time for half an hour and then his clients would start rocking up not long after that. The place Lance was renting didn't have a peep hole to see who was knocking. It was coming together. Old Lancelot figured he had it all sorted out, ripping off a pathetic-looking choof dealer. 100 per cent profit, you beauty. Little did he know that I was watching his every move and it was all about to get very real.

My plan was to catch him off guard early in the morning and smash him in the nose. Any time I've been hit hard in the nose has been an awful experience. The pain shoots right up into your brain and fucks you up, there are tears in your eyes and you can't see a thing. There is a period of about thirty seconds when you are rendered useless and all you can do is wait until it stops. This would be the perfect opportunity to give him a sound thrashing, maul this motherfucker right from the get-go and not give him one chance to think or speak.

At 9am the next day I walked up to Lance's front door with my heart beating like an African drum and adrenaline coursing through my veins. Even though I felt exposed and unprotected my energy levels were driving me to test myself against the unknown, there was no way I was going to back down from this situation. I had psyched myself up and no matter what happened with this altercation Lance was not going to get on top of me. Even with all this running through my mind, I felt a strange serenity travel from the base of my spine and up my back. I was relishing the emotional turmoil and it was staggering how this feeling got me higher than any drug I have ever experienced.

I knocked on Lance's door and it seemed like my heart was now in my neck. No answer, so I knocked again—I figured he wasn't used to getting out of bed for anyone at this time, so he would be groggy and disoriented. Then I heard some stirring and footsteps, it was go-time baby.

He opened the door about 5cm and I went *whooshka* and kicked the front door right into his face and it smashed into his nose just like I had planned. Lance was a big unit all right, but that wasn't going to matter to me. I got inside and kicked him in the chest with real force. Lance went flying into the wall behind him, he was holding his nose in agony and I had a feeling it was broken from the blood on his pyjama top. I let a big right hook go and it connected with his temple and the top of his cheekbone, not a great punch, my hand was killing me. It did do the job though and he was staggering and completely unsure of what was happening. I grabbed him by his top and threw him into his lounge room. Lance went crashing into his coffee table, the bong water went everywhere.

I noticed Lance's German shepherd was going bananas and I could see him jumping up and down through the glass sliding door. It's pretty useless having a big scary dog like that if all he can do is watch his owner get the mother of all arse whippings. I kicked the shit out of Lance, working his ribs and kidneys, then I jumped on his head two or three times—I didn't want to kill him—I just needed him to feel fear. Then I grabbed his hands away from his face and punched his head three or four times. Lance was fucked, he wasn't really in a state to understand, so I waited a little bit until I knew he had come round and I asked him if he knew why I was there. Turns out Lance did know why I was there, so I smashed him again with my right fist and landed it right on his lower jaw. I was really enjoying the power I had over him. In my mind, I justified this by telling myself that he owed money and had done the wrong thing. But, truth be told, I was like a dog that had tasted blood for the first time. I loved the carnage and the power. It made me feel great.

I explained to Lance that what I needed was the money for the choof. Then I went on to explain to Lance that I didn't trust him and that it would be easier if he gave me the money for me to give to my associates. Lance didn't disagree, which was a sound business decision on his part. I followed Lance closely as he hobbled to his room, just in case he got some funny idea that he might grab a weapon and try to exact some sort of revenge. Lance was completely battered and bruised, there was blood all over his mouth and shirt and no chance he would retaliate, but I didn't want to take any chances. He grabbed the money from his cupboard in two separate piles and handed it over to me, his eyes looking down the whole time. I loved that feeling. I knew that fear only too well. I had been on the receiving end of it and it wasn't a great place to be. I confirmed that all the cash was there and he nodded. Poor old Lancelot just wanted me to get out of his house.

Once I had hopped back in my car, I let out a guttural roar. I felt like I was the king of the jungle. I was shaking but totally energised. Throughout the whole experience, I felt in complete control. In time, I learned the importance of getting in first when you are involved in any hand-to-hand combat. Get in first and make it hurt. There must be so much pain inflicted on the other party that they will do anything you want. This experience fed my ego the way I imagine a supreme leader or dictator would feel. It felt incredible, even though deep in my soul I knew it was cruel and vicious. I didn't care, the adrenaline overtook my moral compass at a rate of knots and I wanted to feel that way again.

The way I appeased my conscience for the evil act I had just committed was by remembering that Lance had done the wrong thing by another party. I was just retrieving the funds. This justification was convenient for the moments of reflection and remorse I would later have. But those moments were fleeting and when I began to think about the power and strength I felt earlier that morning, it all washed away.

After the incident, I contacted the Choof Chariot and squared up the outstanding cash. It would have been easy for me to keep the pay and tell them both to fuck off—truth be told they wouldn't have done a thing. What I did is look at the bigger picture: these two were definitely going to need me in the future and chances were they would recommend me to other people they knew who needed debts collected. This is how the debt collection arm of my business was created. Pubs are amazing places of business for a lot of Australian males. You would be amazed at how many deals, both legitimate and not so legitimate, are organised. Pubs have been productive for me over the years and the idea of a bit of business over a cold schooner gets me excited even now.

When you begin in the underworld, no one has any idea of who you are or what you are capable of. It's like applying for a job as an eighteen-year-old with nothing on your resume. Word of this job spread like a case of crabs at a contraception-free swingers party. Lance ended up telling some people about a madman that jumped on his head and punched the fuck out of him in his lounge room. He embellished the story to make himself look like a victim and this was great for me, as the story was exaggerated over time. The Choof Chariot told everyone about 'The Hammer' and his ability to get it done. Happy days.

GREED

'Greed, in the end, fails even the greedy.'
— Cathryn Louis

The one time I worked in a crew or a gang was a memorable experience. It allowed me the foresight to never ever be part of that sort of arrangement again. When you are working closely with a group of people in an illegal activity, you are at the mercy of the weakest link and even if you have the knowledge and understanding to foresee imminent danger, it doesn't mean the gang will listen to you. With so much ego, testosterone and one-upmanship at play, it became clear that success would be nothing but a pipe dream.

The self-appointed leader of the gang was Carlos' cousin, Chewy. He had been struggling to get anything cooking for a long time and was in desperate need of a head start. I set up a meeting for Chewy and another drug dealer, under the proviso that Chewy would befriend the drug dealer and begin doing business with him. This was all under false pretences. The main goal was for Chewy to build some trust, rip off this drug dealer when he felt the time was right and, hey presto, he would have some startup capital and we would all begin making money together. Chewy did the business and the unsuspecting dealer was robbed of a nice little earn; he was small fry in the scheme of things and regarded by Chewy as collateral damage. What was the dealer going to do—go to the police? I don't think so.

The idea was for the earnings to be split among our team of five people, but right from the start Chewy said he would just hold onto the cash and keep it in a safe place. The writing was on the wall for me right here—Chewy had no plans of letting go of this cash. His whole demeanour began to change now that he felt like he had control over the rest of us. It was staggering how Chewy's temperament had gone from a fun-loving guy to a narcissistic, self-absorbed beast. This was the critical juncture where I decided that as soon as I could get away from him, I was gone.

I had recently taken some ecstasy on consignment from a Greek bloke I knew and the balance needed to be fixed up, so I made sure my share of the earn squared up the balance to the Greek. Chewy was filthy when he had to hand over my end of the cash, I could see the jealousy in his eyes and the need to control was eating him from the inside out. In reality he couldn't deny my request, I had set up the rort and it was only fair I get my share of the payday. It proved to be a masterstroke on my part as Chewy's greed was about to bring the whole thing crashing down.

We had been doing some bits and pieces for a while as a team: moving speed, ecstasy, cocaine and choof, but because of the way Chewy had structured the kitty no one really knew how much we were making and this was playing right into Chewy's hands. Any time we questioned him about the grand total, he would say that everything was written down and we would divide it all up when we reached a certain figure that always seemed to be out of reach. This really began to give me the shits, so when Chewy loaded us up with the substances for a Saturday night, I decided I was going to enjoy the spoils of my hard work and spend all the profits. I ended up having an absolute blinder and went large at the VIP room at Room in Hawthorn. I had moved a heap of pills and powder at a mate's presidential suite hotel room and we all ended up back at Room nightclub. I shouted people drinks and lines of cocaine, having a hell of time and when it came time to weigh in the next morning, all I had was the money to cover the merchandise. That's right, I had spent every dollar of the profit right down to the last cent. Chewy was disgusted with me for two reasons: the first was I had a great time with what he perceived as his money. The second reason was the he couldn't do a damn thing about it. I was effectively thumbing my nose at Chewy's rules and regulations regarding this imaginary kitty and even though our gang gave me a solid grilling, it all blew over and we continued to work together.

About a month after I got massive at the Room nightclub an interesting opportunity presented itself in the way of a vigilante group. The group I am talking about was a loose collection of young men that had been in and out of jail for stabbing, robbery and generally creating chaos across Melbourne. They were well-known for sticking up drug dealers and stabbing them with a ferocious determination. Their fearless leader, a bloke by the name of the Lizard, was about to be released from the boob and the group wanted to make sure they had a massive party waiting for him when he got out.

Basically when the group were outside prison they went on a crime spree; robbing dealers and taking any drugs they could get their hands on. The group would stay awake for days, their mental wellbeing a touch on the unstable side. When it came to violence this group of adolescent males were not afraid to get their hands dirty. Blood and guts were their specialty and this separated them from all the other two-bob pretenders I had come across.

Our point of contact with this group was a bloke called The Monster. The Monster was a street-level junkie incapable of sitting the right way on a chair. Like all junkies he lied like a flat fish and when he made decisions, heroin was the thing he put at the top of his priority list. The Monster thought it was funny to put unsuspecting people into a room where they couldn't escape and pull out his syringe and pretend that he was going to stab them with an infected needle. The Monster had no intention of following through with it—he just enjoyed watching the fear in people's eyes. He tried his bullshit with me one night and I picked him up and threw him on the floor half a dozen times. The Monster never bothered me again.

The Monster looked like Agro from *Agro's Cartoon Connection* and he had this laugh that went on and on. His father was a fall-down drunk and when you have a role model like that, I guess you are always going to be kicking into a ten-goal breeze. Because of his heroin habit, the Monster had come into contact with a lot of undesirable characters. The Monster was not really part of their crew, I guess they liked to have him tag along for good humour. The thing about a bloke like The Monster is you can never underestimate how dangerous a simpleton like that can be and all our lives were about to be thrust together in a strangely bizarre set of circumstances.

One Friday night our gang were together at a house in Bentleigh planning our events for the weekend, when Chewy received a phone call from The Monster. I couldn't hear exactly what was being said, but I did pick up that there was a real sense of urgency. I had a feeling that this phone call was going to end badly. As soon as Chewy hung up he explained to our gang that the Monster was with the group known for stabbing people and they had ripped off a drug dealer for a large amount of ecstasy. The group was looking to offload the merchandise. Chewy had taken it upon himself to organise a meeting near McKinnon station with The Monster to hand over a large amount of our money for their loot. What could go wrong?

The Monster had set the trap beautifully and Chewy was about to fall right into it. Chewy's ego had determined that the group would never dare rob him and the promise of a large amount of cheap ecstasy had overridden any suspicion he would normally have had. Greed was making all the decisions for him and we were all about to learn a valuable lesson. No one said a damn word to Chewy about the chance of these maniacs turning their knives on us, all Chewy could focus on was getting the cheap ecstasy and turning that into profit for the imaginary kitty.

We arrived early to survey the place. The plan was for Chewy to park opposite the station and wait for The Monster and one of the group to walk over and complete the transaction. I was to wait around the corner in my car with another member of our team. If anything was to go wrong I would fly round the corner and rescue Chewy. As we both sat there in my idling car waiting in the darkness, it was obvious to me that we were about to be on the receiving end of what Chewy had dished out to a previous dealer.

The Monster walked over to the car with a tall, skinny junkie. The junkie got behind Chewy in the back seat and The Monster sat beside Chewy in the front, then all hell broke loose. Blokes started coming from everywhere and Chewy was in a world of trouble. The junkie behind him put a massive blade straight to his neck and went to slice it open. Chewy had the presence of mind to grab his hand and stop him. The junkie demanded the cash and Chewy had no choice but to hand it over, the group had the car surrounded and it was at this point that I came flying round the corner and proceeded to drive straight through the crowd. They all scattered pretty quickly. I pulled up at Chewy's door and he jumped out of his car and into mine. When I saw the bloke that sat behind him jump out of the back seat with a large knife I locked my door. All I could hear was The Monster screaming, 'I've been shot, I've been shot', which was nothing but a distraction. In the heat of the moment it created the perfect decoy for the rest of the group to slink away into the darkness.

We booted out of there as quickly as we could and I asked Chewy what had happened. He explained that one of them tried to slit his throat, which is a stark reminder how cheap a human life can be in a situation like that. We cruised round the block and Chewy wanted to head back and make sure his car was still there. It was, so he jumped back in it and we headed to a safe place down the road to discuss our options. Chewy was filthy at his inability to read the critical signs of this set-up and later accused me of being weak for locking my door. I didn't give two shits what he thought about my actions under pressure, he was the one who led us to the slaughter. We knew then and there the money was gone, one of the other blokes on our team wanted to drive around the different train stations looking for the gang, but I told them all they could do that without me. I'm sure all the members of our gang thought I should have joined them, but for me that was the end of our relationship. Never again would I be at the mercy of someone else's decision making. I could see this all unfolding before it happened and I couldn't do a thing about it. This gang I was running with were focused on being the big dogs of that area and I didn't see any point in being well known in an area I had grown up in. Bentleigh is a beautiful area to raise a family, it's not exactly rich with knockabouts. That was it for me, I was on the large now and expanding my enterprises and entrepreneurial skills in other suburbs.

BETTINA

'You're my favourite bad habit.'
— unknown

It all started innocently enough at the VIP room at Room nightclub in Hawthorn. This was around the same time as the incident with the marijuana dealer. Bettina was sitting with her girlfriends and I was snorting lines off my own table like a real attention-grabbing big shot. Even from where I was, I could tell she was an outgoing girl with a bubbly personality; she had a Penelope Cruz thing about her, so I went over. Bettina and I got talking and she explained to me that she had been in a relationship for six years, but the passion had evaporated. I ended up exchanging numbers with her, on the proviso that if they needed any party favours she would give me a call.

That same evening my phone rang. Bettina invited me over to her place—her bodybuilder boyfriend had gone out to work. I had a strong suspicion it wasn't for a cup of green tea. On the way I got some cocaine for my journey out to Kensington. By the time

I arrived I had hoovered half a gram of the white stuff and I was feeling optimistic about my chances of creating some magic with the lusty Bettina.

I knew this girl had some designs on me, I could feel the energy. There was something about the chemistry between us. Whenever I looked at this girl I just needed to have sex with her. As it turns out, she felt the same way.

I walked in to find her watching *Pretty Woman*, her favourite movie. I sat down on the couch next to her and pulled out the bag and started lining up on the coffee table. I offered Bettina some but she declined and mentioned that she had a terrible headache, then she walked upstairs without saying a word. This threw me into a weird space—here I was watching Richard Gere trying to straighten out a sex worker and I was the one on the couch, high on cocaine with a rock-hard erection. Next thing I knew Bettina invited me upstairs to keep her company—well that was more like it. The electricity between us was undeniable. Bettina undid my pants, jumped on top of me and began to ride me like Seabiscuit. Halfway through our romp Bettina started to feel guilty and jumped off me saying, 'We shouldn't be doing this.' I diplomatically agreed with her, but in the back of my mind I knew the seed had been sown. We ended up driving around together and going to different nightclubs and enjoying each other's company.

Bettina was a restless woman who enjoyed the attention of men. She fancied herself as a bit of a fashionista and her appearance meant the world to her. She portrayed an image of confidence, but deep down she was a very insecure little girl.

We ended up going to Chapel Street one day and we clicked. It was a nice day, but I had a migraine and needed to lie down on a park bench. We wrapped things up and I dropped her off at home. Her boyfriend was waiting for her and he was a monster of a bloke, a big bodybuilder who bounced at a few nightclubs. Bettina told him I was gay so he didn't get jealous. We began a messy affair that went on for three years. It was the wrong thing to do, but I was young, inexperienced and the idea of an attractive girl choosing me over her partner pumped up my ego.

We snuck around and did all that stuff you do when you're having an affair. It was exciting and outrageous at the beginning. But after a while it began to wear thin, her boyfriend was onto us and she had to come clean.

It is important to note that at this point of my life I was a complete coke head, I was so caught up in the idea and image of cocaine and the way it made me feel that I began to lose myself. I was doing some business with some serious people and that, in itself, was like a drug. Everything I did revolved around drugs.

Once Bettina admitted the truth to her boyfriend, it was time for her to move out and find a place of her own. This was disastrous as Bettina had no idea of how to manage money and neither did I. During this time, we moved in with her sister and her fiancé in Keilor. The Western Suburbs is an interesting place but definitely not for me.

Now that we sort of had our own space, we embarked on a tumultuous partnership founded on jealousy and mistrust. When you begin a relationship on the back of an affair, there are elements of toxic energy that can overshadow all the good qualities. For example, if one person heads out for a night with their friends, the other person begins to wonder if they are really going to do what they say. Being young and coming from a place of inexperience, communication wasn't strong. Fighting and making up was more or less what our relationship entailed so, for the next few years, that was our lot.

There were some great times in-between, we did love each other. But I was so concerned about Bettina cheating on me, I decided to get in first and take a piece of every woman I had the opportunity with, on the odd chance that she was doing the same. I am pretty sure she had her fun as well.

I drove her crazy; I was completely out of control with my need to take drugs and have a good time. That came first and foremost, everything else ran a distant second. I would go out for hours at a time, sometimes even days. Then I would rock up at home like nothing had happened. Bettina would go right off her 3KZ and I would have to make serious reparations.

I always knew she would take me back. I was a real shit like that, the original fuckboy. I thoroughly enjoyed watching her get all worked up, she would scream and yell at me. Sometimes I boiled over: I might smash a TV or break her hair dryer. The hair dryer was a regular victim, this really pissed her off. Then I would hide her make-up and this would push her right over the edge. The police were called once for our domestic dispute. The whole thing was volatile; we brought out the worst in each other.

Together we were a bit like Bonnie and Clyde, a couple of immature kids leaning on each other and trying to navigate our way through life. Even with all this I look back and smile at the thought of us together. Thank God we had each other—no one else could deal with us.

RIPPED OFF AT MACCAS

'Hell is empty and all the devils are here.'
— William Shakespeare

The one and only time I was ripped off involved the son of a mafia boss and a heap of cocaine. I will call the son Enzo. Enzo was in his fifties and was a slick operator. Enzo looked exactly like a mafia boss; he was short and thin with a direct confidence and an insatiable love for drugs and dirty sex. I had known Enzo since I was about four years old; he was the dad of one of my good mates. We reconnected at my mate's twenty-first birthday and had been doing business together ever since. Enzo loved cocaine and he had recently called me to say he had some new gear that was incredible. The coke Enzo had given me was A-grade, it was an amazing product. This was still when Bettina was with the bodybuilder. The bodybuilder loved coke and made a big order, so I organised for Enzo to get me some decent volume. He said that wouldn't be a problem. I teed it all up with the bodybuilder to meet me at Maccas in St. Kilda for the transaction. Enzo lived round the corner and wanted to meet there. The bodybuilder and I met in his car, I grabbed the cash off him and told him to sit tight while I went over to see Enzo.

Enzo was edgy right from the start, we didn't meet in his car like we normally did—he was on foot. He asked for the money first, which was also unusual, so I gave him the big wad and he reached into his leather man satchel and grabbed a fist of white powder wrapped in a plastic lunch bag. Enzo put it in my hand and then bolted off into the night. I walked back to the bodybuilder's car, gave him the merchandise and we parted ways.

Later that night Bettina rang me to say the bodybuilder wanted me to know that the package was caster sugar, not cocaine. This was not a good situation. I called the bodybuilder and told him I would make sure he was paid back in full. I jumped on the phone to Enzo but he was not answering. I had been ripped off big time. The kicker was that I couldn't do a damn thing about it, Enzo was a connected guy and I was a nobody, I was still too green. He had set me up right from the start. The coke he normally had was average at best. I had tried it plenty of times, enough to get you going, but no real kick. Then all of a sudden he has this amazing mind blowing stuff at a cheap rate. Enzo used my naivety against me. Here I was thinking he was going to look after me, we had known each other for years, after all.

It was a harsh lesson for me; my ego took a real hammering. I was twenty years old and it turns out I didn't know everything. The saying goes: 'Remember that life's greatest lessons are usually learned at the worst time and from the worst mistakes.' From this experience, I gained a keener sense of what I needed to look out for. When I looked back at all the signs and Enzo's body language, it made sense. It was an Academy Award-winning performance. He played me like a violin.

I paid the balance back to the bodybuilder eventually and we sort of caught up at a much later date. I apologised for doing the wrong thing with Bettina and the money. The bodybuilder was a good dude; he was an understanding man.

As for Enzo, I ended up bumping into him at a nightclub,

he was with a gorgeous blonde and some serious gangland personalities. He was paranoid I was going to make a scene in front of his gangster friends, so when I walked over he put a whole lot of cocaine in my hand. He gave me his number and I caught up with him a few times, he squared up most of the cash he owed me. Then he got pinched for commercial trafficking. Enzo ended up doing seven hard years of prison.

Enzo did his time and didn't rat on anyone even though the police offered him all sorts of bargains. He didn't say a word, that's why he did such a huge sentence for what he was pinched for. They wanted him to help them with another, bigger, matter but old Enzo kept his mouth shut. Then he got out and vowed that he had changed and wanted to live the quiet life. There is no doubt that seven years would change a man. Enzo died of a heart attack less than a year out of prison.

I GO ALRIGHT AT THE DISCOTHEHQUES

'If you want to be a party animal, you have to learn to live in the jungle.'
— Lisa from Weird Science

The Chief was first introduced to me by a retired AFL footballer whom I will call Lips. Lips introduced me to the Chief at the Vineyard late on a Sunday night. 'This is the Chief, he is the ex-CEO of so and so and he is responsible for this and that.' I shook his hand and asked 'How's that working out for ya?' From that moment on the Chief and I were best mates. He asked me what I did for work and I told him that I went alright at the discotheques. The friendship was odd to say the least. Here I was, a twenty-two-year-old sociopath determined to carve a career out of Melbourne's underworld. And then you have the Chief, a thirty-six-year-old, ex-CEO of a massive Australian company. The Chief had a $350k Amex expense account, business connections all over the world and a thirst for drugs superseded only by me. The Chief had recently divorced from his wife, his love of drug-taking was a big reason for that. The Chief was a private school boy who had never indulged in that side of life. So to hear that it was his wife who had given him his first pill, then left him because of his addiction, is ironic.

The Chief was fairly fit from all the drug-taking. I have seen photos of him before and he was a gigantic business bodied slob. He was just over six-foot and intelligent. His dry wit and comedic timing were impeccable and because of this we were inseparable. We bounced off each other, the connection between us just made sense and for the first time in my life I found someone that got me.

The Chief and I went on one of the most interesting journeys, as we developed and learned off each other. Lips said to me at dinner one night, 'With the Chief, if you keep your ears and eyes open you are going on an exciting ride my friend.' To be able to be plugged into the subculture of society that the Chief moved in was valuable. Though not all of what I saw was conducive to the way that section of society likes to portray themselves. It was a real eye-opener, my exposure to the 'Toorak set' strongly confirmed the belief I had in my own path. I realised that if you can be successful playing the game by their rules, the game didn't stand a chance.

With the advice and guidance of the Chief, I gained a new perspective on the way life can be lived. I took the Chief to all sorts of places and he did the same for me. It was hilarious to see the Chief at Bubble, Zos or the Viper Room, shirt off, pinging like a bitch. He loved it, I had unleashed the beast within. We would both go in and have a quick squirt on the dance floor. He was very flexible like that and he took to the dance floor with aplomb. Can you imagine that an ex-CEO rocking it to hard trance, fucking gold. We were kindred spirits.

It really was an incredible time. After partying with me for a few months The Chief rang me one day to tell me he had spent $50k partying with me in a few months. Here was I thinking, 'You used to be a CEO so you have that sort of coin'. I was just twenty one and I had blown more than twice that over the same time!

THE PRELIMINARY FINAL STORY

'When the going gets weird, the weird turn pro.'
— Hunter S Thompson

The morning of the 2002 preliminary final, Collingwood versus Adelaide, was one of the more bizarre starts to a day that I have had. The Chief and Dmac came over to my house in Hampton to pick me up in Dmac's Saab. Dmac was the only bloke I have ever met that drove a Saab and to say the Saab suited him is an understatement.

They arrived at my house a bit earlier than expected; I was in the process of getting ready to have a shower. So just before I hopped in the tub, I used my signature move to fuck the Chief and Dmac up, in a way that the both of them will never forget. I put a big pile of ketamine on the table and said, 'Go for your lives boys'. By the time I got out of the shower, the pile had nearly gone and the two of them were sitting at the table snorting and trying to clear their noses. I giggled, the Chief was still very green when it came to drug taking etiquette. He also had no idea how hard he was about to be hit by the k-hole.

The effect of ketamine is a reduced sensation in the body, giving you a floating or detached feeling, as if the mind and body have separated. Some people feel incapable of moving, which has been linked to the near-death experience called 'entering the k-hole'.

On our way down Hotham Street towards Richmond, the Chief showed his first signs of some wear and tear. He began moving really slowly and saying some particularly strange things. This began to concern Dmac who was now entering the early stages of his own k-hole. His main concern was that the Chief was driving his Saab. I was in the back watching these two dickheads trying to navigate a straight line. Dmac began to become stressed because he realised the Chief was experiencing exactly what he was feeling. Between the two of them, they decided it would be a good idea to pull over and let me drive. Pulling over when you're battling the effects of horse tranquilliser is not an easy task.

After much deliberation, they managed to get the nose of the car up on the kerb. As soon as this happened the Chief lay back, like he had been hit by an elephant bullet from a sniper rifle. He then realised he needed to throw up the contents of his breakfast. The wrestle to unhook the Chief's seatbelt began. The Chief attacked the seat belt with much intensity but he just couldn't get it to click and open. Defeated, he sat back in his seat, arms down by his sides and head tilted all the way back. Dmac was also completely fucked but he didn't want the Chief to chunder all over his Saab. I watched these two, with tears in my eyes.

Eventually they worked together to release the seatbelt and the Chief ran over to a tree and grabbed on for dear life as he projectile vomited his breakfast on Hotham Street. This proved to be the last straw for Dmac who nearly started crying. He demanded that I stop laughing and go see how the Chief was. When I got to the Chief he was holding onto the tree and leaning backwards like a water-skier. It was as if gravity was pushing him backwards. I had to compose myself and then I leaned into the Chief's ear and said 'Hey Chief, enjoy this mate, because you will probably never get to be this off your head ever again.' With that, I walked back to the driver's seat and waited for him to finish. The best part is that we were guests in one of those catered boxes at the MCG.

I managed to get us to Richmond, where I parked the car and the Chief began to come around. The good thing about ketamine is it doesn't last for too long, so I rolled up a note, put it straight in the bag and had a blast myself. I don't remember anything until after half time, which was great because we were average until then. When big Anthony Rocca kicked that bomb from the centre square to bring the house down, well, I went off-tap in the box. When we eventually won the game I had one foot out the box and was giving all the Adelaide supporters the chainsaw as they left. What a great day.

DINNER FOR TWO

'Poor soul, you were just too high strung'
— Doc Holliday from Tombstone

As with anything in life, when you get some experience under your belt, you gain confidence in your ability. When you believe in yourself you become better at whatever it is you are doing. When you get accomplished at things, your reputation precedes you and people talk about what an amazing job you are doing. It's human nature and debt collection is no exception. I had reached a point where my presence was enough to get the person or people I was chasing to immediately reconsider their bad judgement. Occasionally I would have to find someone that didn't know anything about my activities. I would ring them up and tell them that I needed to see them about an outstanding sum of money. If this person fancied themselves as a knockabout, they may tell me to go fuck myself. When I would hear this, I would get very excitable because they obviously didn't know my reputation. Then I would make it my business to find out everything about this person and slowly undermine their bravado. Death by a thousand cuts. I would leave notes at their homes or with their wives and partners. I would call them late at night on private numbers and breathe into the phone. My favourite way of completely unhinging the mark was to knock on their door late at night after a barrage of this sort of treatment and leave. Sometimes I would hide out of sight and listen to their reaction at my knick-knocking ways. By the time I would finally catch up with them, they would beg for the treatment to end. I would punish them physically and mentally. The beating I would hand out was the tip of the iceberg, there may have been months of mental disintegration that came before the final coup de grâce. I had nothing but time on my hands and I really loved fucking with people.

What really empowered me, was when I forced the person I was after to cry. I just loved watching anyone at their threshold or breaking point, it used to really get my heart pounding. In a way, I felt sympathetic to their plight, but on the other hand, I wanted to take them way past their vulnerability. When a person would break down and cry I would not say a word, they thought by showing me this emotion I might stop what I was doing. But I had seen all this behaviour before and I genuinely enjoyed watching the way different people reacted under pressure. For me it was similar to watching the way people run, some styles are so unusual you can't help but just stare. I am an emotional person and I cry all the time, mostly over an inspiring or happy moment. The thought of crying through fear or pressure fascinates me, so anytime I dealt with a person going through the cut and thrust of a tearful adventure, I did my best to ensure they got it all out of their system. I would question them and get them to talk while still emotional and there is nothing more humorous than watching a person trying to communicate when they are crying their eyes out.

There was this guy named Ed who ran a successful restaurant in Toorak. I knew Ed long before he became an entrepreneur. He was a tall fellow with a lean build, receding hairline and a set of eyes that were reminiscent of a man that had something uncomfortable inserted into his anal passage. Real bulbous eyes, like a possum. When word got around about Ed's dynamic cuisine, the Toorak set were all over it. My old mate Ed was doing a roaring trade and business was flying, he began to make all these new and well-heeled friends that introduced him to cocaine, horse racing, exciting business opportunities and Ed began to get in way over his head. The cocaine Ed was now snorting on a daily basis changed the man and he became quite tardy with some of his suppliers that looked after his restaurant.

One supplier was a well-respected Italian fruit and vegetable personalit who was well known at the Footscray Markets. Cocaine is a sensational drug; it has the ability to redefine your entire existence. Now, the Ed I knew would never underestimate a supplier and replace his better judgement with a new found love of cocaine. But that is exactly what Ed did and the gentlemen from the Footscray Markets always gets paid one way or another, so he let Ed's bill run up to an extraordinary figure.

When the Italian identity decided he wanted to cash in, he contacted me and asked me to recover the folding as Ed was not returning his phone calls. I went ahead and left an urgent message with him to call me back, but nothing came. So I rang the restaurant and tried to get him there but Ed was always busy. It was clear to me he was ducking a few suppliers and never answered the phone. Being the caring and understanding type I reconsidered my approach and booked a table for two at the busiest time on a Saturday night. If Ed didn't have me, an old friend trying to recover the cash he owed the Italian identity, he may well have ended up in the boot of a car and dumped in one of those deep holes up in the Macedon ranges that a few bodies are rumoured to be thrown down.

What I did was engage two intimidating individuals to go and dine at his establishment. Patty, the big Irishman, is 6'7" tall with tattoos all over his body. I'm talking neck tattoos, the whole fucking shooting match. Patty has a goatee, shaved head and looks like he rides a motorcycle for an outlaw club. He can also fight like a threshing machine and once took on and disposed of the entire security team at a place called Wild Bills at Southland in one spectacular evening of unbridled violence. I love, and still associate with, Big Patty. He is a dear friend and someone I consider one of the most loyal people I know, a king among men. The other bloke I sent is another 6'7" unit from Airport West called Jonno. He used to run a security gang that specialised in cleaning up rough Painter and Docker pubs before there was professional security. Jonno was fantastic with one-on-one combat and was accomplished with all sort of martial arts weaponry. He is another ripping chap that I still see regularly and regard as a good mate. These are the sorts of blokes who, when you see them walking together, you look the other way, not the sort of people you would expect at a fine dining establishment in Toorak. This is precisely why I sent both of them to scare the hell out of the Toorak scene on a busy Saturday night at Ed's restaurant. I made sure the two of them wore clothing that showed their tattoos and sinewy physiques. You can only imagine the sort of attention these two received when they sat down to peruse the menu. From all reports a lot of the clientele were so aghast at the presence of my dear friends they upped and left. Others began questioning Ed about their motives and when he walked over to discuss this with Big Patty and Jonno, he approached with fear and trepidation.

My mates had been worded up and told Ed, 'The Hammer has sent us both to enjoy an evening of opulent dining and we are keen to stay here all night.' Well, Ed jumped on the phone and called me straight away and then I had the opportunity to discuss his outstanding invoice with a certain fruit and vegetable supplier at the Footscray markets. Ed knew about the exorbitant bill he owed the Italian, but didn't realise how much business he would lose while my friends were dining in his establishment. He didn't know how much respect the Italian evoked in people. I went on to explain that my friends were going to come back night, after night, until his business was full of my buddies keen on an indulging experience at Ed's expense.

Ed started crying even louder now and begged me to call the heat off. I told him they wouldn't be going anywhere until they had been fed and the money he owed the Italian was handed over. Ed was clearly at his threshold, he managed to get some food out to the boys and went to the safe and grabbed all the cash he had to give to Big Patty and Jonno. The cash wasn't all there, but come Monday morning the remainder was fixed up. Ed was better for the run. I'm not quite sure what ended up happening with my old mate and the restaurant business, but I do know I saved him a world of pain with the Italian and if you are reading this Ed, you owe me one.

WHAT A YARRA

'A pheasant one day, a feather duster the next'
— Charlie Wootton

I was contacted by a couple of Chinese gentlemen heavily involved in illegal gambling and drug distribution throughout the city and the western suburbs. These men were not the type of people that you take lightly, they both had fearsome reputations for getting things done and were extremely low key in the way they handled their business. People that failed to meet their demands seemed to vanish. I will call them Mr. Wing and Mr. Wong. I met the two of them at a quiet restaurant in Chinatown and I knew from the start that if I accepted the job there would be no allowances for mistakes on my part.

They were afforded their own personal table and the owner of the restaurant made a special effort to please the two of them and anyone in their company. Mr. Wing and Mr. Wong were both slight men with immaculate attire; they both wore understated designer clothing that reeked of good taste and money. Underneath those clothes they had artwork scripted all over their bodies. My friend that put me in contact with Mr. Wing and Mr. Wong had given me a debrief on where they both sat in the food chain and how I should handle the two of them.

When I arrived, Mr. Wing motioned for me to come to their table and the owner of the place made a big fuss of my presence, which I thoroughly enjoyed. He ushered me to their table and kept bowing his head in such a respectful fashion that it made me feel important and I couldn't help but think that I could get used to this sort of treatment. We shook hands and sat down, the owner took my Versace jacket and vanished. One thing I did notice was there weren't any menus on the table. Mr. Wong asked me if I would like a drink and I told them I was happy to follow whatever the two of them were doing. Mr. Wing and Mr. Wong both spoke to each other in Chinese and then nodded to the waiter, who immediately brought over three glasses of top shelf Courvoisier. As I sipped my drink I was trying to guess how old both of them were. I figured they were between forty-five and fifty, their mannerisms and body language oozed confidence.

I was careful to be on my A-game, but I also wanted to show them the respect they had treated me with. I had a feeling that Mr. Wing and Mr. Wong were watching my every move. Mr. Wing motioned to the waiter and the food came out. We started with soup and went on to eat about six courses of the most magnificent Chinese I had indulged in since I was last at the Flower Drum. The Peking duck was out of this world. I had to do my best to eat with some sort of decorum, my natural tendency is to destroy anything put in front of me with great haste. We talked football and then I worked the topic of conversation onto horse racing, which I knew would be a favourite with these two. When I mentioned my first ever big win on the horses, they both began to relax. I explained in great detail how beautiful that feeling was in 1997 as I stood on the winning post when Might and Power romped home to win the

Caulfield Cup. I had smashed that amazing horse with the bookies as a sixteen-year-old and I stood up in the restaurant and showed them both my fist pumping and victory dance. Mr. Wing and Mr. Wong were in hysterics, taking into consideration their placid demeanour, this was a strong sign that a connection was forming between us. I have always had the ability to relate to people and I used it to my advantage that day.

What was supposed to be a brief meeting ended up being quite a long lunch, Mr. Wing and Mr. Wong got stuck right into the drink and I followed suit. We were all very merry by the last course and they suggested I come with them to a brothel they had a piece of. We went right on with it into the evening with some gambling at another place they were involved in. It was at this point I suggested we get the business out of the way and with that the two of them straightened right up and put their game faces back on. Mr. Wing asked me to leave my phone on the table, then they both stood up, as did I and we walked into the kitchen and then into the stainless steel cool room to talk. Mr. Wong patted me down for a listening device and the business began. Mr. Wing explained to me that an associate and family friend of theirs had a brother that had been viciously assaulted for no reason at a gambling den. The brother had been beaten so badly that he was now mentally and physically incapable of the basic motor skills he previously enjoyed. I couldn't help but think there was going to be some serious repercussions for that individual in question and for the sake of the story I will call him Terry. Mr. Wong took over and explained that they could not locate Terry anywhere and it was of great importance that they find him, as this was a personal matter. To this day I'm still not sure if they were aware that I knew how to find Terry or they just got lucky with me, Mr. Wing and Mr. Wong played their cards close to their chests. Mr. Wing noted that they had heard good things about my ability to find people that didn't want to be found and then they mentioned the figure I would receive if I was able to provide them with the address. The figure was huge and gave me a clear understanding of how much they wanted to find him. Mr. Wing and Mr. Wong didn't want me to be violent, they just wanted the address and they would handle things from there.

This was a personal vendetta and I could not have been happier with the arrangement, but I had to play it cool and make out like I was pondering the difficulties of the project. I asked a few run-of-the-mill questions as we finalised the details. This job was a gift from the gods—I happened to know Terry's friend Spider, shaking that prick down for an address was not going to be a problem. I told Mr. Wing and Mr. Wong I would need a week to get the address and we organised to meet up at the same restaurant at the same time in one week. No talking on phones or discussing anything. They were over the moon and, even though outwardly they made out like they were cold as ice, I could sense Mr. Wing and Mr. Wong felt like they had struck gold.

We left the cool room and I declined their offer of brothels and gambling for a later date. I explained that it was more important to get the business completed and then we could enjoy the finer things in life, to which they both smiled at and nodded to each other. It was a productive afternoon and even though there was no mention of what would happen to me if I couldn't get it done, the underlying menace was there. You see, anyone operating on this level doesn't have to act hard, they just are. I was aware of how important it was for me to nail this job and if it wasn't such a simple task I would have declined the offer, no matter how big the purse was.

Terry, the bloke they were chasing, was your typical razzle dazzle wannabe gangster; extremely violent when he had people behind him, but deep down Terry was a bonafide coward who slept with the light on and sat down to piss. This was going to be enjoyable. When I was an up and comer, Terry treated me like a coldsore and he didn't even know me, that was just his way. If he could stand over someone, he would. Terry thrived on intimidating and controlling people and since the incident with the brother, Terry had gone to ground and no one could find him. All the bluster and bravado had evaporated and he was now jumping at shadows, which is really what Terry deserved, that sort of stress shaves years of your life.

With a job like this, and I say this because there was a solid amount of money on the table, it was imperative to use people with a proven history of handling pressure. So I decided to call two Albanian brothers I had known for a long time. The biggest mistake a lot of people in this line of employment make is involving external parties that aren't up to scratch. Either they are greedy and try to save as much of the payday for themselves or they legitimately don't know anyone capable enough to handle themselves under pressure. These types are consistently brought undone and boy, do they pay the price when it all goes wrong. For me, the most important part of any project was doing things by myself. But if I did have to outsource, I made damn sure they were the best people money could buy and the two Albanian brothers, Massi and Sunni, were just the type. Massi and Sunni were more than capable. With guns and extreme violence, it's vital that you don't go into a job with people who go over the top, as this can bring you undone faster than a greyhound chasing a hare. You need people who have been involved in extreme situations who know what needs to be done. You can't have an imbecile straight from jail thinking he is Rambo and let shots go all over the place because he is nervous and trigger happy. I had worked with Massi and Sunni before, to hire these two didn't come cheaply. But they were calm under pressure and this suited the work like an Iced VoVo at an afternoon tea party.

We all met at the beach for a swim to discuss the requirements for the job—when you're swimming any listening devices are rendered useless. Not that I didn't trust these two, I just liked to be safe. Massi and Sunni were intimidating. They were both mountains of man with hands like ham hocks. They carried the expressions of people that had lived in poverty and survived. As we chatted in the water, I explained very little about anything. All I needed them to do was drive a car and hang a person off a bridge till I got the information required. Massi and Sunni burst out laughing at the idea.

It all took place late on a Saturday night. The person that knew of Terry's whereabouts was Spider, a law student with a penchant for cocaine and the good life. Spider was an obnoxious human with no redeeming features whatsoever. I made some quiet inquiries earlier that week and Spider was all set to be at the Q-bar that Saturday night.

I got Massi and Sunni to park round the corner and I walked into the Q-bar, which was a miracle in itself. The manager Richard had been told that I had previously been terrorising patrons and shaking the bar in the VIP room. It took a handwritten letter from the son of a well known socialite family in Melbourne saying that I was a close personal friend of his and I should be let in to repair the damage. When I got in I found Spider trying to dance with a drink in one hand and a nice-looking blonde on the other. Spider smiled when he saw me and gave me a big hug, he was coked up to the eyeballs, which worked in my favour. I told him that I had some amazing gear in the car and we should go and snort some together. Spider loved the sound of this and gave the girl he was dancing with his drink and assured her he'd be back soon. Like fuck he would, Spider was in for an interesting Saturday night.

We walked around the corner to where Massi and Sunni were waiting in a nondescript Toyota Camry. When Spider got in the back seat, he still had no idea that we were going to test the strength of his web slinging abilities. 'Hi guys, I'm Spider. I'm a mate of The Hammer here,' he said, and the Albanian brothers started giggling like school boys. I had to keep a straight face. Massi and Sunni already knew the bridge we were going to hang Spider off and started making their way there, still, Spider had no clue what was about to unfold.

When we arrived at the spot we parked in the darkness and we all got out. Spider was the last to get out as he thought we were going to snort some high-grade cocaine. Before Spider had a chance to say anything Massi and Sunni grabbed his legs and upper torso and began walking to the middle of the bridge. Spider quickly realised the enormity of the situation and started asking me what was happening. I explained that we needed to have a little chat and the bridge was the best place to do that. As the Albanian brothers hung Spider over the bridge by his feet, Spider pissed all over himself. Spider started explaining that he hadn't done anything wrong. I told him I needed the address of his elusive pal, Terry.

It hit Spider like a tonne of bricks. I could see in his upside down facial expression that he was caught between two Albanians and a cold river. 'I can't give him up Hammer, he will kill me' said the Spider. Then I went on to explain that it was his problem. I also explained that I had no intention of telling Terry who gave me the address and I was sure there were people lined up to find out that information, it was only a matter of time. Spider, to his credit, didn't budge. Now when you're hanging someone off a bridge by their feet it is only a matter of time before someone sees you and realises that this isn't a couple of blokes having a good time. So I nodded at Massi and Sunni to let go of one leg and sure enough, the Spider was more than willing to offer the address up. The image of him hanging from the bridge by one leg looking like, well, a spider was something I will never forget. No web slinging or anything. The Albanian Brothers were giggling so hard they nearly did drop him in the drink.

They pulled him back over the ledge and walked him back to where our car was. Massi pulled out his shooter and got Spider down on his knees, then pointed it straight at his head and demanded his driver's licence. Massi explained, 'If you mention this to anyone, we know where you live.' Spider nodded and gave over the address, I left him on the bank of the Yarra, off his head on cocaine and with piss all over the front of his shirt. The job was done.

Later that week I met up with Mr. Wing and Mr. Wong to hand over the address and enjoy some more of their hospitality with an afternoon of gourmet cuisine, sex and gambling. They were extremely appreciative of my ability to get the job done and when I arrived at the restaurant they had a fat envelope full of crisp, green $100 dollar bills; Mr. Wing and Mr. Wong were fantastic payers.

I squared up with Massi and Sunni and all was well. Except for Terry, he didn't go missing as I thought he might. If I can be so bold as to borrow a line from the movie *RocknRolla*—Terry's indiscretion cost him an arm and a leg.

I never did any more business with Mr. Wing and Mr. Wong, it didn't feel right. I kept them as friends and very handy contacts. We socialised a fair bit and they are some of my staunchest allies.

Spider, well, Spider found God and another state to live in. From all reports, he is a law abiding citizen and I have no doubt that evening helped him get there.

MY OTHER ADDICTION

'I like threesomes with two women, not because I'm a cynical sexual predator. Oh no! But because I'm a romantic. I'm looking for 'the one'. And I'll find her more quickly if I audition two at a time.'
— Russell Brand

Any young male teenager will tell you: when the hormones start to kick in all you want to do is get your end in, it's as simple as that. I watched the guys I knew sucking up and doing whatever young girls wanted on the off chance they get an off-cut thrown their way, but that behaviour was not in my DNA. I was never going to be a submissive pushover. What I did was save up some money, ride my bike down to the Daily Planet and I chose the woman there who most looked like Pamela Anderson. It was truly a breathtaking experience for a fifteen-year-old to lose his virginity to a mature woman with experience and knowledge of the male erogenous zones. I had no idea you could feel that way. To top it off she gave me a massage at the end of it.

I gained some really handy tips from a professional about how to please a woman. From that moment on I have always been with older women, always. At seventeen I was with a twenty-three-year-old, at twenty I was with a thirty-year-old and at twenty-three I was with a thirty-two-year-old. I didn't see the point in wasting time with young girl problems. With maturity comes experience and when it comes to sex, I am all about experience and women who know what they want.

Blokes who struggle with women have me baffled. In my experience I have found some ladies love a bit of spunk, they love the truth even if it gives them the shits and they love bad boys. I happened to tick all three boxes and that wasn't good luck or a fluke, I adapted, changed and evolved. I paid women attention and lavished them with expensive gifts and weekends at fancy hotels. The choice for them was made easy. Think about it, if you were a woman would you rather go to a nice restaurant, have a respectable amount of red wine and go home for some nice sex? Or would you rather book the presidential suite at the Como and have wild crazy sex after snorting lines of cocaine off the grand piano, then head to the VIP room at the best nightclub in town and drink champagne until the morning, then wake up and have another crazy sex session and go shopping for the day? If you were a nice girl, then I would try my best to corrupt you and many times I did.

There was crazy hot sex in the back of cars parked on busy freeways, sex in the middle of parks in broad daylight and torrid love affairs with mature women. It was spontaneous, unbridled and completely out of control.

There were orgies, swinger's parties, two ways, three ways, four ways. There isn't much I haven't done with the ladies. This all felt normal at the time and when I look back I'm glad I got it all out of my system when I was young; no stone unturned sort of thing. A lot of the time I wasn't even looking or interested in women and I think it turned them on even more, how fuckin crazy is that?

My poor girlfriend at the time, my God she put up with some

stuff. One particular time, I told Bettina I was popping out for a bit. A bit, turned out to be the whole night and I was still going. The problem was I had to go past our flat and grab some more ecstasy to keep the party going into the next day. Bettina was going to be fired right up. This was proving to be a tricky situation, because I also needed to keep moving. There was another girl waiting in the car. I ran the gauntlet. Bettina started going off her head at me for not coming home, so I quickly ran for the stash, grabbed the business and ran out of the flat into the car.

For the women it was always fun and fleeting, they knew that. I was always clear: Bettina was the girl I lived with and loved. But I would always get a case of the wanders and drift past some of these ladies' houses on the way home to Bettina, afternoon delight sort of arrangement.

Occasionally I would drop off some party favours to a girl's house and they would pull me into their bedroom, next thing you know my pants are down and I'm getting choc-a-block. Once I got a touch of the guilts and had to stop mid-stroke and go home, all I could think about was Bettina.

Upon reflection it is clear now that I was addicted to sex. I had a partner but I was going to sex wokers, as well as having affairs. Asian, African and European women: big, small, tall, busty, petite, mature, it didn't matter, I was insatiable. Not only was it the excitement of different women, it was the adrenaline of getting caught that I thrived on. I was being hunted and the little vixen Bettina would go to all lengths to try and catch me. This was the most entertaining pursuit on the planet. Same with the police, I loved it when I knew they were following me. To give you an idea of how unbalanced I was, Bettina and I might wake up and have a romp, then I would head out and go to the Daily Planet. I would get a case of the wanders and drift past Port Melbourne to see a woman I was having an affair with for a bit of hush makundi and on the way back home to Bettina's I would slip into a parlour for a massage. Sometimes I would go to the same girl at a brothel, two or three times in one day.

At the time it was way out of control and I didn't understand why I was doing it. There were times when I would be driving along, completely unsure about why I couldn't be a normal person. Sure it was fun and my experience certainly helped me to understand how to satisfy women. There have been many times that women have complimented me for my voracious appetite in the bedroom and I enjoyed the feedback. I was a rock star and I revelled in being a Lothario.

THE AWAKENING

'When your back is to the wall and you are facing fear head on, the only way is forward and through it.'
— Stephen Richards

At this stage of my life I was twenty-three years old and had been involved in the underworld for about three or four years. I was flying off the reservation and running red hot all the time. The way it all panned out, I ended up doing some business with the Persian, a dangerous career criminal. Because of his capabilities and willingness to take things to next level, the Persian had access to huge quantities of illicit substances at amazing prices. Anything from drugs to guns, the Persian was able to facilitate my growing shopping list. We ended up doing a few things together and I received a huge quantity of MDMA in powder on credit. The Persian was a dark-looking man, always moving fast, like he was trying to out-run life. Our lives intersected at just the right moment for me to learn a truly valuable lesson.

Things were going swimmingly. I had met the Chief and

the Toorak set and we were partying like it was 1999. My end of the agreement with the Persian was okay, I had covered most of the money I owed him. It's what I had given out to two certain people that became the problem; their slice of the action was never recovered. When it came time for payment they couldn't be located. The Persian wanted his money and I didn't blame him. He called a meeting and I asked him for one more day, hoping that would be enough time for me to find these lecherous peanuts.

I was filthy at myself for letting the situation get this tight, partying with the Toorak set and relying on other people were two crucial learning points in this experience. You never rely on people in the drug industry, that decision changed my life forever.

In the end there weren't any more excuses I could make, the Persian knew I didn't have the splash. My fate was to be decided at a meeting in the afternoon, in a back garage of a mansion on Dandenong Road in Malvern. This wasn't the sort of meeting where you have a cup of tea and an assortment of cream biscuits. I was going to face some form of physical violence and there was no way to avoid it.

It's incredible how heightened my senses were, I can remember everything. As the Persian drove me to the house I felt a huge bit of phlegm caught in my Adam's apple and it wouldn't go down. The thought of pain had crossed my mind but didn't scare me. There was no one else to blame, I would have to accept whatever punishment came my way.

The Persian kept re-adjusting something in his sock, I should have known it was a gun. My focus was on his three mobiles phones that did not stop ringing during the drive. The Persian was dangerous and busier than a one-armed paper boy. It was an awkward car trip, I was obviously on my way to be disciplined for not having all the money and the Persian was the executioner.

The Persian parked the car and we walked to the back shed of this property, three other young guys like me were all waiting in this dark and dingy room. The room smelt like old carpet and bong water, there was lots of graffiti on the walls and old rolled-up carpet underlay was lying on the dirt floor. Bang, one of the young blokes smashed me in the face, no blood at this stage and a pretty average punch. Bang, again from another one of the young guys, this punch was much the same as the first. I should have just pretended to be hurt and dropped. From what I gathered in my short time in the back shed was that the three young blokes were supposed to be learning the art of violence. By me standing up to their punches, it made them look incompetent. The Persian looked at these muppets and sighed, then smashed me in the forehead with the butt of a 9mm Beretta. It was instant stars, like in the cartoons and a loud ringing. The feeling of cold hard steel breaking the skin of my forehead is not something I will ever forget. I was surprised that I was still standing after this blow, so when I saw the Persian pull his hand and gun back for another swing. I fell over real fast and the Persian's glancing blow grazed the corner of my eyebrow.

As I rolled around in the dirt to avoid being hit, everything slowed down. This is what my life had come to. The Persian stopped swinging the shooter and started pointing it at me and I stopped rolling around immediately. I knew he wasn't going to kill me, but there was a massive chance he might shoot me. He pointed the gun straight at my head and asked where his money was. When I explained what had happened, he started demanding I tell him where these people lived. I didn't answer. Even though I was on the ropes and the people that owed me the money had split, it didn't mean I was ever going to be a dog. This simultaneously infuriated and impressed the gang, the idea that I was a rock-solid operator saved me from serious damage. The Persian pointed the pistol at my legs and asked me if I wanted one in the leg. I remained silent.

In the end they picked me up and dusted me off, one of the blokes walked with me out the front and gave me a smoke. It wasn't till then did I notice all this blood had run down my face and onto my shirt. My head had been opened right up, there was a big hole in my forehead where you could see bone. The bloke laughed and said that the wound was a good one. He also commended me for not giving the other two peanuts up.

The Persian drove me back to my car and we agreed on different payment terms. During the drive back to my car, he was talking on the phone to one of his minions about how much damage they had caused to someone I knew. In hindsight it could have been really bad for me, luck had definitely been on my side. They had destroyed this other bloke, and I mean destroyed. I saw him after and he was in terrible shape, he couldn't walk properly for a long time. Gas, as he was known, was black and blue and disfigured. He has since passed away.

This was the moment that made me realise nothing good comes from pretending to be something you are not. I had pretended to the Persian that I was capable of covering the money but in reality that was complete bullshit. I was relying on things going perfectly to make all the money back. It was during this period I had fallen in with a bunch of people that had money to burn. This behaviour had come home to roost. Some might think it's a harsh lesson, others might think I got off lightly. For me it was probably a bit of both; I needed a reality check. If I had continued the way I was heading for much longer who knows what may have happened.

The experience helped me evolve as a person. It wasn't that I was completely over the darker side of life. I revelled in my infamy. It was more that I was one step closer to making my way back to the person I wanted to be.

NIGHTCLUBS,
THE DRUG BUSINESS AND HOTELS

'Freedom is wild, and to be free we must at times live dangerously and wildly'
— Bryant H McGill

I have always wondered if the public know how many lives the Crown Casino has affected. When the casino was built, it created a vacuum. Men who ran casinos in Melbourne, the underground versions, all employed security; there were men in the underworld hired strictly for this purpose. You needed a certain type to make sure other crooks don't get the idea they can run through a place of business. This was employment for blokes that would probably struggle to find employment anywhere else. Mainly because of their records and the way these men appear. When the Casino opened everyone in this scene became redundant.

With a bunch of people unemployed and set in their ways, they needed a revenue stream to feed their families. They moved onto the next, quickest way to make fast cash: shifting illegal substances. This created an influx of people on the streets dealing drugs and creating havoc.

The new casino became a breeding ground for criminals to meet, do business and launder money. By the time the police became aware of this activity, the damage was done. Sure, the police are onto it now with taskforces and bans on nefarious characters. I am good friends with one of the old boys who ran the main card games, back before the casino became the go-to place. The bloke reckoned that the casino lacked personal touch. He said, 'No one went home empty-handed. You see, the old way, everyone knew each other and if a bloke had done his balls, we were never going to send him home to his family empty handed. He would always get a sling to cover him for the week, the gambler was a valued customer and there was a relationship.'

The damage the casino has done to the everyday families of Melbourne can never be questioned. So many people have lost homes, people have lost their families, businesses and, some people, their lives. Whenever I drive past that place I get this uneasy feeling, it's like a man-made cancer tearing at the fabric of our society, similar to the pokies. But there are handy taxes and tariffs that the government rely on, if only they would open their eyes and look to the future. The revenue to be made off legalising drugs would outweigh any of the bullshit they collect from speeding fines, gambling, tobacco and alcohol.

The thing is, when laws change, it is indirectly going to affect someone and it's impossible to predict how. The casino was a massive mistake—sure it employs people and that is great but the bad that place does for our city far outweighs the good.

Fancy hotels are another amazing by-product of the drug scene, they go hand in hand. Between Carlos and myself, there aren't many hotels we haven't stayed in. It was the done thing. If we started campaigning early on a Friday, one of us would book a hotel so we could set up shop and go hard. That way if people needed anything they could just meet us at our spot, I never let anyone back to my house at any stage of my career. The convenience of a hotel was fantastic, a mobile office. Carlos and I would get into the hotel robes and slippers, then we would look out over Melbourne, like kings.

The Robbie Williams Room was the presidential suite at the Como hotel on the corner of Toorak Road and Chapel Street. The room had two levels, a twenty-person jacuzzi, a grand piano and a Bang and Olufsen sound system. It also cost $1300 a night back in 2002 and we had it for a few nights. I was running ecstasy from Sydney to Melbourne. I had made a bit of money over the summer and New Year's was set to be a blinder. There were about six of us and we had so many pills and so much powder it was ridiculous; we were double dropping grey melodies every hour on the hour. This whole bender cost me about $6000.

Chewy and Carlos were snorting speed and heaps of it, Bettina was upstairs in the jacuzzi watching *Goldmember*, flying on the grey melodies as well. The stereo was rocking. It was a wild night. We partied straight through the night and into the next morning. By now we had at least twenty people come to the hotel and nobody had Summerdayz tickets. The plan was for Carlos and I to head down early to see if we knew someone there who could get us tickets. On arrival there was a girl we knew working in the booths, Carlos went over and ordered twenty tickets and then he turned to me and said 'Hammer, I need $2000'. Without even thinking I threw a wad of $2500 over so he could grab the tickets for all of us. It wasn't till I watched everyone in the queue eyeball the wad of cash flying into Carlos' hands did I realise how out of control we were. This was not normal behaviour, I could tell by the way people were staring at us. Most of them had never seen that sort of money before and here I was throwing it around, literally.

We all headed back to the hotel room with the tickets and partied on all day.

The whole gang ended up rocking at Summerdayz in epic fashion, we were young, cashed up, drugged up and having a massive time. We danced so hard that evening, it was one for the ages and even now when I think about the fun we all had on the dance floor it still gives me goose bumps.

We ended up taking the night over to the Q-bar and rocked it there for a bit, then we wandered back over to the presidential suite and went hard. I snorted so much MDMA that I needed tissues to hold in the powder in my nose. My nostrils were dry and I couldn't keep all the powder in so I inserted tissues like tampons into my nose. It was madness, there were beautiful women on the bed, my younger cousins ended up coming as well. Imagine being eighteen and experiencing this shit, people in the jacuzzi, drugs everywhere, just help yourself.

The next day Bettina and I woke up and went shopping, we bumped into Johnny Jet-ski driving down the street. We told him about the hotel and a whole bunch of people came over. Johnny Jet-ski brought over some cocaine and we all started campaigning again.

For three day we lived completely in the moment. No one gave two shits about anything other than having fun and getting off our heads. There was nothing like it, everyone relaxed and dropped their egos at the door, there were no inhibitions.

GOLLUM AND THE VINEYARD

'Excuse me if I don't shake hands.'
— Doc Holliday from Tombstone

There was a fella I knew, who was called Gollum because of his strong resemblance to the character in the *Lord of the Rings* movie. Gollum was a skinny, malnourished-looking specimen, with enormous eyes and very little hair on top of his head. Gollum liked to talk a lot and this included talking to the Victorian Police, which is a cardinal sin if you are involved in drug dealing. Very much like the character, Gollum was a survivor. I received reports from a Romanian crook I knew that the safe as houses Gollum had been pinched selling dope and opened up like a can of worms back at the police station. He was relaying information to anyone who would listen in a vain attempt at self-preservation.

So when this information flew across my desk, I contacted a couple of business associates I knew who were very keen to hear of Gollum's activities at the cop shop. When something of this nature happens, it's extremely bad for business. Anyone who has been involved with Gollum or is doing business with Gollum has to shut up shop or run the risk of being locked up. If you choose to run the gauntlet and continue with your regular routine it comes with a price, so most people shut up shop and this means you are not earning any money. Some people are smart and put a nest egg away for this situation; they might go on a holiday. But many don't have the financial nous to manage this and have to keep doing business. Dangerous times indeed and it's not that Gollum was some big drug baron; he was a minnow in the scheme of things. The underworld is a house of cards. There is no stability and a snivelling underpants gnome like Gollum can create havoc if he decides he wants to put himself first, which is exactly what he did.

The two gentlemen met me down at the park and I relayed the information I had heard to both of them. These two weren't small fry by any stretch of imagination, one was manufacturing speed and the other was the prime marijuana grower in the south-eastern suburbs. So for these two, this sort of information was vital, it may have meant the difference between a lengthy jail sentence or worse: losing their entire business. Both of these blokes weren't surprised at all—Gollum made you feel a level of uncertainty when you were around him. The two of them thanked me graciously for letting them know and explained that if I ever had the opportunity to square up with this cretin, there would be a pay day in it for me. This was all well and good, but I mentioned to the boys that Gollum would be hard to find for a while as I had no doubt he would go into hiding and wait until this all blew over. Either way, these gentlemen explained it didn't matter how long it took, they wanted it squared up.

I kept tabs on Gollum over the next couple of years. After his conversation with the police, it seems Gollum had gone towards the straight and narrow, which is great for him, but there was still some karmic debt to repay after his confessions to the boys in blue.

Flash forward three years, my mate Buck and I were smashing

down schooners at the Village Belle in St Kilda all afternoon and it had been a lovely day. The pub has a great view down Acland Street and we were enjoying the company of a few backpackers we had attracted with our Australian charm. It was now heading into the evening and as a group we decided to continue with our soirée down at the Vineyard. As we walked down Acland Street I could hear Buck telling these backpackers his wonderful tales of the country and the Australian outback. Buck was in fine form and had the ladies eating out of his hand with his laconic drawl and little Johnny jokes. All this socialising was about to change in the blink of an eye though because when we arrived at the front of the Vineyard, my precious, Gollum himself was walking out.

'Hey Hammer!' yelled Gollum at the top of his voice. Bang—I spilt Gollum's forehead open like a watermelon with a thunderous head butt. He had blood pouring from this wound; Buck went straight from Russell Coight-mode to Buck-mode and got stuck right into the rest of his crew. I knew it wouldn't be long before the team of Islander bouncers at the Vineyard would come over, so it was important we kept it brief. After all, this was right out the front of a heaving nightspot at its busiest time. Onlookers were horrified to watch the violence unfold while they were sitting out the front sipping on long necks.

Gollum had the chicken dance going as he staggered towards me. I told him I knew he was an informant, then I let go with a short and sharp left-right combination that had him reeling. Then the security guards came from everywhere targeting Buck and me. The situation spilled out onto Acland Street and the traffic had to stop. The most important thing for me was to keep Buck safe as he had no idea this was about to happen and that wasn't fair on him. I made sure Buck was behind me and we both walked back slowly away from the throng of muscled up Maoris. The two of us didn't stand a chance against eight of them. We knew they just wanted us away from the venue, we were bad for business.

Gollum was a mess, he was in the arms of his new friends who were none the wiser of his history. No doubt they were commiserating with him over the senseless attack from a couple of bloodthirsty psychopaths. He had blood all over his shirt and it looked like he would need quite a few stitches from what I could see. Now that is a square up.

Buck was pissing himself all the way home and when I finally explained the reason for the *tête*-à-*tête*, he was happier than a beaver in a wood yard. Buck then went silent and asked where the girls went and we burst out laughing. Buck is such a staunch friend and I love him dearly for it, he was straight into it. What a champion.

On Monday I rang the two gentlemen three years after the initial meeting and asked them to meet me at the Elsternwick Hotel for a beer. When we all met, I explained what happened to our dear friend Gollum and the two of them had to hold onto the bar they were laughing so much. I knew they would enjoy it. The two of them went to pull out some folding to pay for my services. But I told them that was a favour from Buck and me. I didn't need the money and it's better to have people like that owing you, not the other way around.

What a lot of people don't understand about that world is that for the pretenders like Gollum it's fleeting fun and more or less a vacation. But for the people that have grown up in crime families and it's all they know, well, they don't forget about things so easily. They are entrenched in that way of life. So if you do the wrong thing and, let's face it, Gollum had done the wrong thing, there will be repercussions. You can bank on retaliation no matter how long it takes. They will wait years for retribution and I can guarantee you by the stunned look on Gollum's face out the front of the Vineyard that evening, he had completely forgotten about his indiscretion.

THE POLICE CD

'Blessed are the peacemakers, for they will be called children of God'
— Matthew 5:9

One night I was out and about when the phone rang. I was about twenty-four or twenty-five at this stage; nearing the end of my underworld career. Carlos was on the other end—he said, 'I have something here you are going to want to have a look at'. By the tone of his voice, I knew it was going to be serious. I certainly didn't expect it to be an official police CD with twenty recorded tracks and myself on three of them. Carlos just played the patrs I needed to hear and even though it was clear I wasn't the main target all I could think was 'how did this CD come about to start with?'

Scratchy was his name. He looked like a smaller version of Biff from *Back to The Future*. Scratchy was a pathological liar suffering from bipolar and he was a gambler with little to no control over his addiction. On top of all this Scratchy was from Bentleigh, our old area, so Scratchy had the hook he needed to start friendships with Carlos and me. He was going to turn our comfortable lives of luxury on our heads.

Scratchy had a red-headed younger brother called Itchy and they were both loose cannons. You couldn't trust either of them to sit the right way on a chair. Itchy was solidly built and crazier than his soft-hearted brother, he fancied himself a bit of a tough guy. In truth the two of them made an entertaining duo; they were as mad as a clown's cock.

Scratchy was into me for about $10k at one stage, he thought of me as a bank. People would ask him for drugs and because he had this idea of himself ruling over Melbourne, he would get the drugs off Carlos or me. Then Scratchy would go and gamble his profits and our share of the business. He was one of those secret gamblers that you never actually see spending any money. When I had a meeting with his parents to discuss a payment plan, it came out that he owed money to everyone. There was an orderly queue, it was out of control.

I knew from the moment I saw him starting to dag around the places we hung out that everything was going to change. It was clear to me—Scratchy was a shooting star, they burn bright but not for very long. He would stalk us all and conveniently rock up to the venues we were at. How are you meant to deal with an individual like that? 'Hi guys, have to stop running into each other like this. Let's just exchange numbers and be best friends.' Because I am a sucker for entertainment, I welcomed the drama. I knew this bloke was going to bring us all undone at some point and I decided to use that as the opportunity I needed to take a step away from the scene altogether.

Scratchy thought he was a persuasive orator. He used this skill to his best advantage. He would land himself in some amazing positions; the Brownlows or in the pits at the Grand Prix with the grid girls. He was talented like that. The thing was that Scratchy thought he would be able to use the same skill set he relied on: his mouth. Only this time in a much more dangerous game. We warned him at the start not to get involved, Scratchy was a visionary and had some huge dreams he wanted to achieve. All I could do was look on.

Itchy was always trying to hassle me to get him drugs. The couple of times I did, there was always a drama. He would always be short with the cash and he would make me chase him for payment. This bothered me. One day I bumped into Itchy after a long time and he grabbed my number and started ringing me incessantly. Itchy was still striving to be a big shot. He explained that he had this amazing cocaine and he should bring me some. I wasn't going to disagree with him. If someone wants to give me cocaine, then that's fine with me. What Itchy didn't realise was I was going to take his cocaine and not pay for it, as a square up for all the bullshit he used to put me through. So I told him to bring me about $2000 worth, I tested it on the spot and it was amazing. Perfect. I told Itchy that I needed to go and give it to a bloke and grab the cash. Poor old Itchy was apprehensive about this for a good reason; he could sense I was going to rip him off. He should have listened to his instincts.

Anyway the days went on and I didn't ring him or pay him a cent, poor old Itchy rang me hundreds of times a day. First he would send me aggressive messages, threatening me with harm. I wouldn't reply, then he would try a different tact, Itchy would be nice and matey with me. 'C'mon mate, let's catch up and have a beer'. That sort of thing. I wouldn't reply to this either, so Itchy would ring again and I would answer and be really happy and positive with him. Itchy would nearly be in tears from frustration and the fact he knew he was being played. This went on for a week, till I told him the gear was a present from him to me and everyone else I shared it with. He deserved that one.

Itchy was also the bloke that found the Police CD in Scratchy's bedroom. When he saw it he grabbed it and rang Carlos. Carlos listened to it and rang me. I was taken aback to hear myself, loud and clearly talking about a commercial quantity of ecstasy on a recorded CD compiled by the Victorian Police. Turns out our mate Scratchy was into sound production as well. It all started to make sense. Some reasonably serious people received jail sentences around the time Scratchy burst onto the scene. There was mention somewhere along the line that he had an uncle who was a cop, surely this couldn't be him.

I ended up being very close with Scratchy, he revealed all his challenges to me and I'd like to think that I was a supportive friend to him. He was a loveable bloke; humourous with an infectious personality. Our friendship was built on truth and honesty. Some of the experiences Scratchy shared with me were deep and emotional. He did explain to me one day the song that best described his life was *Unwell* by Matchbox 20. My heart broke for the bloke; he was genuinely a great fella but he had his demons. Scratchy was desperate to break onto the scene with drugs, wild sex parties and nightclubs. He just had no idea about the strict rules you had to follow to keep your head above water and from the moment he entered the pool he was trying to get some air.

Now it is clear to me how easy it is to fuck up in that life, to survive a year in that landscape you need to have decent smarts about you. I have heard people say that drugs are easy money—that is some delusional shit. There is nothing easy about that way of life. You are always looking over your shoulder and watching your back. It's a 24/7 job. It's survival of the fittest.There is getting caught by the police and doing time. There is getting ripped off or disposed of by some up-and-comer who has seen *Casino* way too many times. Scratchy had no experience—he figured he would be fine.

By this stage Carlos and I had our own crews in operation, consisting of around thirty people to move stuff and organise different jobs. The landscape changes constantly, the bigger your immediate circle of influence the easier it is get things done. Scratchy saw this and decided he would organise his own crew—this was always going to be a disaster. Scratchy was a talker, not an organiser and he certainly wasn't a financer, so the best role for him would have been getting potential investors to the table. Scratchy had some important ideas in his head and I'm pretty sure those ideas involved him sitting on a throne, with a crown.

At first I thought it was a coincidence that Scratchy used to pop up at all the same nightclubs, bars and pubs as us, but after a while it became ridiculous. We would be at the Q-Bar and Scratchy would be there by himself, then we would all shoot off to Seven and Scratchy would rock up there as well. Because he was so new to the whole scene, he didn't have full control of his body or face when he had taken illicit subtances. He would never stand at the bar or dance like a normal person. He'd hug the velour robes on the walls of a joint with a head on him like a Cheshire cat, or he would stroke the walls and smile like he had an erection as big as his forearm. Scratchy loved getting off his head, he just had no control over himself once he did. I loved it. I found Scratchy to be great company. I would point out a few minor players on the scene and a week later Scratchy would be mates with them, it was incredible how quickly this bloke moved. Scratchy was one of the keenest, most driven dudes I have ever met. He was always going to leave a big imprint wherever he went, so I figured I would tag along for this explosive ride.

One of the flats Bettina rented was a place on Alma Road, St. Kilda. This joint was a drug taking temple. It was conveniently on the way to Chapel Street and St. Kilda so it was perfect for anyone going out and about. I only invited Scratchy over to that place for the first time when we were moving out and I told him this as well. He wasn't a trusted member of my team, by a long way. But I allowed him to be in on small projects. He would beg me to introduce him to some of the bigger people he was obsessed with. Much to my amusement, Scratchy still thought the whole thing was easy. So he continued trying to climb a mountain that was completely out of his grasp. Scratchy progressed with childlike ambition, nothing was going to get in his way. He still had a long way to go in my book, but

I always kept him close so I could monitor where his head was at.

One time I pointed out an old Melbourne identity called Con. Con was a wrestler back in the day and now has a security company that runs the door at The Prince of Wales. What do you know, less than a week later, they became friends as well. Scratchy decided he would run the door at the Prince of Wales with Con. Now I must be clear with the fact that his new role as the dual doorman for the Prince of Wales was a self-appointed, non-paying role. He didn't ask anyone for permission, he just started doing it. Con just laughed. I think he liked Scratchy as well. Con allowed him to stand there and allow different people he thought were solid performers on the scene. You can imagine our faces when we get to the Prince of Wales and Scratchy is saying yes or no to the patrons. It was insane, at no point did Scratchy ask for permission, he just worked his way in there. It was a real gift.

From this moment on things were tropical, you could feel there were people watching us. Scratchy was a big personality and big personalities attract attention. He couldn't avoid it. It was his greatest asset and also his worst foible. Now we began to be exposed to people that were out of our control and this is where you begin to leave yourself open.

It wasn't long before one of Scratchy's new associates brought some heat from the police. This bloke had one of the loudest canary-yellow GTS Monaros, he was begging to be pinched. The Police nailed this bloke and on the CD that Scratchy had in his possession, I was on a few of the phone calls speaking in the background about figures. They started following Carlos and I everywhere, just like drama always followed Scratchy.

One time he tangled me up in this mess with the bikies, he so badly wanted to be involved in something, I let him talk me into one medium-sized project. He said he could get ecstasy tablets at an insanely cheap rate, so he wanted to use my contacts with these violent people to sell some. What could go wrong? He ended up getting half the pills and getting shafted for the other half. The bloke gave him duds, now the bikies had fronted me the cash and it wasn't till I dropped them off and they tested the purity of the MDMA in front of me, did I realise how fucked we were.

I wasn't normally on the receiving end of a rort. The bikies were really good with me at the start, they told me I had a certain period of time to come up with the cash and it was more than fair. The way I handled the situation was by telling Scratchy he needed to come up with a portion of the cash or they were going to cut his head off in his sleep. He drove me to the meeting, so he knew I wasn't mucking around. I slapped a bit of mayo on the story with the head-chopping just to keep him focused.

To cut a long story short, we ended up getting all the cash back for the bikies and I made a fortune off the dodgy pills by getting the runners to dispose of them at the local cattle markets. Scratchy had to borrow money to cover what had happened, he had to get two cash money loans with a massive repayment balloon. He paid them off for a long time. Scratchy learned a valuable lesson that day.

One night we had been at the Boutique, Viper Room and the Q-Bar all night and were snorting coke and having joints back at the Chief's place. Scratchy had managed to land a position there and he was on his best behaviour around the Chief. Scratchy surprised us all by telling us at 9 on Saturday morning that he had to leave and play football. The Chief and I nearly died of laughter—football in his condition was a pipe dream. Lo and behold, Scratchy lined up on the half-forward flank in the seconds for the Ormond Amateurs. Not long into the football match, Scratchy was dragged off the ground for falling over at centre-half-forward by himself. No one pushed him, he was that off his head he fell over his own feet. He rang me afterwards and asked me if he could come back to the party. He certainly was a character.

I had long left the whole scene but Scratchy got deeper and deeper. I confronted him years later regarding the CD. He said he had no recollection of it, so I reminded him his name was on the front of the CD. Scratchy continued to play dumb, easier to let dead dogs lie I guess. From all reports he dragged himself out of the hole he was in. I heard some disturbing things about him after I left. Now I hear he is doing well in WA with new home packages and I'm rapt for him. It is great to hear he is prospering and I'm sure the distance from Melbourne to WA is what he needed.

I bumped into Scratchy's brother Itchy years later, he told me he had got out of drug rehab, which was fantastic. He looked healthy and had put on some weight. The years of drug abuse had caught up with him a little bit, but Itchy definitely seemed to be a lot calmer and more relaxed.

ISLANDER TO THE RESCUE

'Be the one who nurtures and builds. Be the one who has an understanding and a forgiving heart, one who looks for the best in people. Leave people better than you found them.'
— Marvin J. Ashton

A lesson I will never forget starts with Bettina and me sitting at our house near Chadstone, hungry with nothing in the fridge and no cash. They were really tough times, things were going slowly and the situation looked bleak. There were some forthcoming projects but I had to wait. I had gotten carried away on the weekend with partying and blown all the money for the week. I was banking on some money coming in, and for one reason or another, it didn't happen.

The most important thing I needed to do was get some food, What I did was call the Hungry Jack's around the corner to complain about not getting all the burgers in an order I never placed in the store.

But I had called the Hungry Jack's way down the road, this was a major mistake on my part, I hardly had any petrol. When I arrived at the Hungry Jack's round the corner, the friendly crew explained no one had heard anything about it. I was embarrassed enough as it was, with Bettina waiting for food in the car, so I lost the plot and started yelling. One of the workers heard me say the area of the Hungry Jack's I had called and said that store is further down the road. I apologised and got out of there with my tail between my legs. When I got to the other store the burgers were ready and now cold.

On the way home it was frosty to say the least. Bettina was not impressed with the gourmet food and I couldn't seem to catch a break. I was in the middle of some poor energy, and as I was thinking this, the car ran out of petrol and limped along the highway. Unbelievable timing I looked at Bettina and she was fuming because she knew I was going to ask her to drive while I pushed it into the service lane. When I did, she just moved over the bench seat in the front and started steering; she didn't say a word to me. I remember thinking, she could at least say thank you, but I wasn't brave enough to suggest it.

I pushed the heavy station wagon up the road thinking to myself, 'What am I going to do now? I don't have any money for a cab, no phone or petrol or anything till the next day and we are a fifteen-minute drive from home'. I kept pushing and pushing, then I saw this beautiful, white V8 VT SS commodore slowly pull up next to me. There was a big Islander hanging out the window smiling at me, he said, 'Hey bro, can I give you a hand?' and gave me a massive thumbs up. There was a lovely Islander lady driving the car and I could feel the warmth of their energy radiating all the way over to me.

My position was hopeless, so I said to the Islander, 'No mate, keep going I'm fucked here'. The guy jumped out of his car and helped me push mine into the slip lane. I couldn't believe his act of kindness, when he stood next to me he was a giant of a man. All I could see was his white teeth and this massive smile, his smile made me smile. He had this beautiful aura around him and I felt as if there was something special about him. When we got it into the slip lane he asked me if I had a jerry can—I did but I didn't have any money. So I humbly said 'Mate, you have done enough, I do have a jerry can, but I don't have any money'. He laughed at me again and nodded in the direction of the jerry can, the islander wasn't going to take no for an answer. I jumped into the back seat, grabbed the can and handed it over to my new friend, he laughed again jumped in his beautiful white V8 SS and they both did a burnout as they took off, smiling.

About five minutes later, the Islander rocks up with a now full jerry can and hands it through his window to me. I was really emotional and touched by another act of kindness at a really low point in my life. I was openly crying tears of happiness. What were the odds of finding a person like this? It was like the universe let me know it hadn't given up on me. I grabbed the jerry can and thanked the two of them, tears were running down my face and I must have looked like one hell of a sight. The two of them smiled and laughed with me and when we exchanged the jerry can, the Islander put $50 in my hand as well.

I was blubbering like a young child who hadn't been allowed showbags at The Show. It was all too much for me. Another act of pure kindness. How many people do you know would do the same thing for a drug addict pushing his car up the highway? Not many, that's for sure. The couple laughed and did another burnout as they hooned off. I walked back over to the Falcon to fill it up, with a new outlook on life, as I filled the car with petrol. I realised the two Islanders filled my soul up with their light and the funniest thing is I didn't even get a good look at their faces, just their smiles. I jumped back in the car and cranked it over with some authority. I was back. Then I looked over at Bettina and smiled, she asked what had happened and I explained that an amazing thing had just happened to me.

From that moment on, I never drive past someone who has run out of petrol or is pushing their car, not one. Thanks to the Islander and his amazing kindess, I vowed to do the same for anyone I came across. The flow-on effect from an act of kindness can never be under estimated, this made me feel as though someone upstairs was watching and that was a special feeling.

I leaned over to feel whether there was a burger left for me, there certainly was not. Bettina had knocked them off in anger, which is fair enough to be honest. Then I laughed at her anger eating, it was a good laugh. I probably hadn't laughed like that in a long time, my experience had left me feeling warm and excited. My spirit, soul and energy were really buzzing, the universe had reminded me what it is like to be a good person again.

The future looked different. I was alone and filling up my car in the dark and I began thinking. 'What the hell am I doing, pushing a car, no petrol, no money, no food? What sort of life is this?' I wanted to be the person in the immaculate white V8 VT SS with the mad exhaust driving around doing burnouts and good deeds. I suppose I decided then and there, that's what I wanted to do in life—be kind and help people.

But it was going to take me some time before my head was in a place to put this into action.

CARLOS THE GREAT

'I'm not a perfect person, I make a lot of mistakes; but still, I love those people who stay with me after knowing how I really am.'
— unknown

So many times in my life Carlos was there for me when it mattered and the amount of love I have for that man cannot be measured in words. When my back was against the wall, Carlos was the one constant that I could rely on. He was like a twin brother, so many times we would be relaxing and we would both say the same thing. Often we would be going to do something serious and we wouldn't have to talk, we would both know exactly what we were thinking, like a sixth sense.

We don't see each other anymore but that doesn't matter. I still know how my old mate is and if he needed my help he knows exactly where to find me. I grew up with his family and still hold a lot of love in my heart for all of them. For years they helped me, showed me love and care and invited me to eat and drink at their dinner table. All of this doesn't just wash away because you don't see a person anymore. I never forget kindness like that. The drugs and good times were always going to dry up, along with the people that were attached to them. But one thing's certain—Carlos is always going to be there for me and that's why I have chosen to write a little bit more about some of the more memorable times we shared together.

The story that best describes Carlos' incredible timing took place when we were about fifteen-years-old. We were over at Jessica's house. Jessica was a lovely girl that I went to kindergarten with; she was a real sweetheart and a lover of animals and anything pure. Jessica was one of those people that always did the right thing in life; she still is a class act.

So Jessica was talking to a guy called Digger and myself about her love for cats, when Carlos came in late on the conversation and thought he had picked up the tone perfectly. So the second Jessica finished with her cat story Carlos jumped in with this beauty:

'Haha cats. At my joint my cat pissed in my dad's slipper near the back door and when he put his foot in and felt the cold, he turned around and kicked the cat. The cat hit the back fence on the full.' No one knew what to say, we were all staring at each other waiting for someone to break the silence, when Carlos clicked his fingers and said 'classic.' Then he just walked off, Jessica was in shock and I couldn't keep it together. I ran out of the room laughing.

Loyalty is what matters to me above all. Even before I was involved in any nefarious activity, loyalty was the one non-negotiable I required in a friendship. Many times in my life people have shown me that my non-negotiable friendship foundation was too much for them to handle. I used to think that everyone had the same expectations as me and then I would get hurt when people couldn't show me the same love in return. I began to narrow my friendship group rather than my expectations for a friendship. The people that I was left with, those I could rely on to be loyal and trustworthy, were a small number. My old mate Carlos was top of the heap. Don't get me wrong, Carlos could be shiftier than a rat with a gold tooth. But not with me, we knew each other too well. He knew I needed to trust a person to have them in my life and if I found someone doing the wrong thing, they didn't get another chance. They were barred immediately, no questions asked.

Flashback to the Q-Bar on a Friday night. I was there with Bettina and my mate Jussy—he was the son of one the most violent gangsters in Melbourne in the 70s. Jus could fight like a threshing machine, so we were in good company. There was another guy floating around the periphery called Rory, a big muscular African guy, who fancied Bettina. She had warned me a couple of times that he would go up to her and hit on her when I wasn't looking, so tonight I was onto it. Bettina told me she was off to the toilet, sure enough big Rory thought he would chase her and make a move. I walked over to him and grabbed his massive arm and pulled him up. When you are caught red-handed like that it must be very embarrassing, so Rory asked me if I wanted to punch on. I found this very entertaining. Rory was in the wrong to start with and he decided he wanted to be the antagonist; maybe because he had the big pumped up beach muscles, Rory thought he was a street fighter. I was planning on biting his nose off, when another mate, Troy, came over and cooled things down between us, always the diplomat.

Things simmered between us for the rest of the evening and I could tell his ego and pride had been hurt and he was looking for a way to get his retribution. I saw Rory around town a bit and there was going to be a square-off eventually. Rory was probably twenty kilograms heavier than me in muscle, but this never bothered me when it came to fighting. What I lacked in size I made up for with my wicked viciousness. If you're in a fight, it's the person that is willing to do anything to win that has the upper hand. A large percentage of people in a fight aren't interested in the true blood and guts of good old-fashioned street combat. I loved it and for that reason I was never too worried about taking on a challenger.

The Sunday afternoon after the Q-Bar incident with horny Rory, I rolled up to the Vineyard in St. Kilda to meet Carlos and have a few relaxing drinks. I ordered a long neck and sat down in the corner to wait, when I noticed Rory walk in with about six massive guys. These guys were all well organised; they went to every possible exit and stood there watching and waiting for me. The Panthers made it clear I was the target and it was going to take a miracle to get out of this one. Part of me really wanted to jump on the horn and get a team of people down to the Vineyard to finish this thing off fairly, the Panthers wanted the advantage their way. But I decided to hold my nerve and wait for Carlos. Even with him there, I wouldn't fancy my chances of going toe-to-toe with this crew. There were a couple of these Panthers who looked to me like they didn't really want to be there and I was just as keen to put them to the test.

In a heavy situation like this it's really high-energy stuff, you can almost hear the music from *The Good, The Bad and The Ugly* playing in the background. I couldn't get enough of this feeling, a cross between anxious apprehension and doubled-up excitement and adrenaline. It was the greatest drug of all, working your way through a scenario with ice running through your veins. It's important to be able to acknowledge the threat of physical harm and still be able to think clearly and calmly in a stand-off like this.

When Carlos rolled up, he started laughing, he read the situation blind. Carlos looked at me and said 'watch this', he walked right over to the leader of the Panthers and started having a conversation with him. It didn't take too long before they all walked out of the joint at the same time. Big Rory was left at the Vineyard with his dick in his hand, looking slightly embarrassed. Carlos walked over to me and laughed again. I went and got him a drink and asked him what exactly had happened. He told me years earlier his cousin Chewy and another bloke had destroyed all of the Panther crew at a flat in the Cheltenham area over money. Carlos vaguely knew the leader and mentioned Chewy and the Cheltenhem incident to refresh and reframe the Panthers' memory. The feelings must have been strong because they high-tailed it out of there. Good old Carlos to the rescue again, he was a handy bloke to have on your side.

FLOWERS

'The jealous are troublesome to others, but a torment to themselves.'
— William Penn

It was around this time Bettina and I had really begun to unravel as a couple. I was snorting a lot of pure ketamine and disengaging more and more from my social circle and from life. What I had created was an artificial existence; everything from the drugs to my friends were fake. Even my own existence had become a shambles and I knew it, the ketamine helped me extricate myself from my life.

While most people would take ecstasy, cocaine or speed to feel good and enjoy a high, I was finding escape in ketamine. I didn't need to feel good, I wanted to feel nothing at all.

Waking up one Monday morning, groggy as sailor at port, I indulged in a line to take the edge off, then I punched half a dozen cones and sat on the couch. With breakfast out of the way it was time to plan my day; I was planning on walking down to Chapel Street and grabbing a Boost juice. Then my phone rang—it was

Bettina, we'd had a massive fight on the weekend. The way I saw my life going forward didn't include her and I was at that stage of the relationship where I was looking for reasons to break up.

All I could imagine her saying on the phone that morning was 'sorry'. It came as a quite a surprise when she rang to thank me for the flowers I had sent her. 'Flowers? Why would I send you flowers?' Bettina suggested my behaviour had been sub-par on the weekend. That's when it clicked, the flowers were from someone else. I demanded to know what the note said and it turned out it was from an admirer who worked across the road. It was Chris, a dark and handsome gentleman who had sent them. A friend of Bettina's had mentioned to him that we had been fighting and it looked like we were on the scrap heap, all of which was true. Bettina had always had a way of attracting men. But men with darker skin were her bread and butter, they loved her and she certainly didn't discourage the compliments and advances. I, for one can't blame her; I thoroughly enjoyed any attention from the opposite sex as well.

Dear old Chris who owned a progressive men's clothing label, had locked his sights on Bettina from Scanlan and Theodore. He saw this as a perfect chance to send some flowers and a note saying something to the effect of 'things are going to get better'. Yes indeed, he was a real smooth operator, but he didn't bother to sign it.

Even in my addiction I managed to piece together what was happening. I could recall Bettina mentioning days before a chance meeting between these two and how lovely and positive he was. The warning bells rang for me, so I asked her for the name of the florist. I got onto the woman who worked in the florist, but she refused to hand over the details of the sender. 'It's company policy' she explained.

'Well, how about I come down there and smash your fucking store up?' was my reply to the company policy line,

'It was Chris from his Chapel Street store, now please don't call here again.' Bang, there it was, exactly as I had expected. I rang Bettina back and told her a few home truths. One: she was to get her stuff out of my apartment and two: I was on my way down to Chapel Street to address this issue.

I was fuming and pacing up and down my lounge room in a rage, even though I had cheated on her more times than I care to remember. How dare she flirt with another man. My addiction had led me to an irrational and violent place, a place where my ego and sense of pride were the only things that mattered. The thought of a woman betraying my trust was too much for me to bear. I racked up two lines of ketamine the size of a ring finger and inhaled both of them. Many who have tried the drug will scoff at the suggestion of this amount. My tolerance for pure ketamine was high from abusing it so much. I had purchased a commercial quantity of the drug, not to sell, but for myself. I didn't plan on killing myself when I made the purchase. I needed two massive lines, lines so big that if your average person had one, they would most likely be in hospital. Then I began the five kilometre walk to the corner of Chapel Street.

By the time I got to the old Ardoch Boys school on Dandenong Road, I had to sit down and rest on their fence while the k-hole wore off a bit. I sat there for about five minutes, till the fog lifted. As I marched down Chapel Street, one of Bettina's girlfriends saw me and rang her to say 'He's on his way and he looks furious.' Bettina hid upstairs at her work.

Upon arrival, I noticed that there was a middle-aged woman in the corner with her young son. Chris was conveniently on the phone; I grabbed the phone out of his hand and threw it just past his head. Then I asked him why he had sent flowers to Bettina. He seemed to be stuck for words. So I asked him again, 'Why did you send flowers to Bettina?' Still, he had nothing. So I explained in no uncertain terms, this was his last chance. Chris admitted he thought we had broken up then I just went BANG! With a monstrous right hook that sent him flying into his clothes rack.

It was a huge punch, one of those flush hits that connect superbly with the perfect amount of fleshy cheek and jaw bone, sending the receiver into a state of bliss. The customers hid in the terrified.

Next I walked over and stood in the front door of Scanlan and Theodore and demanded they get Bettina downstairs right away. When Bettina came down she was visibly upset and shaking. We went down the laneway and I explained that we were over and I needed her to get her clothes out of the apartment after work. Then I walked to the Flying Duck and had a couple of pints before walking home.

The most important thing now was to get everything illegal in my joint to a safe place. I rang a mate and told him I needed to stash something at his house. While I was taking the contraband to my mate's safe house, Bettina came in and removed her clothes and belongings and believe it or not she still wanted to come and spend time with me after this incident. She found the whole event intoxicating. She told me she thought the incident was like something out of *Braveheart*. We met up to discuss moving her furniture, but the energy between us was electric, she kept staring at me with those lustful eyes and I could not resist her. When I signalled with my eyes for her to go to the toilets, she got up and walked straight over. Then I grabbed a handful of her hair and pushed the back of her head against the back of the toilet door, I was amazed at how passionate we still were with each other. That summed up our relationship.

Chris, as it turned out, was one staunch individual. He refused to make a statement to the police. He was embarrassed by the whole situation and passed on a message of apology. It's not every day you get to punch a bloke of that calibre.

BARRED FROM CHAPEL ST

'Stalking is such a strong word, I prefer intense research of an individual.'
— unknown

Another major incident revolved around Revolver. I had spent the evening with Bettina and her girlfriends in the city at a nightclub. Why did I continue to spend time with this girl even though I was making plans to move away from Melbourne? That was the only way our relationship was going to finally end. Bettina was now living with her parents but she would come over uninvited at all hours. I could not escape her. The movie *Cable Guy*, when Jim Carrey's character won't leave Matthew Broderick alone, best describes the level of anxiety I was dealing with.

Certain people reading this will be thinking, 'Oh that must be terrible—a beautiful woman coming over in the middle of the night for sex' and yes, I'll admit it was great for a little while. But I can guarantee you, it gets to a point where you start to feel like the walls are closing in on you. I was trying to give up ketamine and get my life together and Bettina, the stalker, was very much from the past. It felt like I was being dragged back into the abyss anytime she was there, even though my energy was focused on dragging myself out of the hole.

Sometimes I would ignore the buzzer and she would go away for a little while. Then she would come back an hour later and *bbaaammpbb*. I feel sick thinking about it now. I have deep sympathy for anyone who has had to deal with a person who won't leave them alone. I felt so helpless, deep down I wanted to go to the police and explain to them what was going on, but what sort of person would I have been to do that to a woman? Bettina just wouldn't give up and this night she had asked me to come with her to a nightclub, mostly because they needed drugs but also because she was struggling with the fact that I had dismissed her from my life. Girls like Bettina weren't used to that sort of rejection.

So here I was, in the club with Bettina and her friends. I had taken a bit of ecstasy and snorted some ketamine, the night was going along nicely. But I was frustrated with myself for being there, it felt like I was sabotaging my progress. We decided to leave and on the way home, Bettina and I had a fight over something silly and I'm sure it was me being ridiculous, I was looking for any excuse to get away from her. The drugs had also kicked in and my mind would have been moving faster than it normally did. So I jumped out of the car and started walking to Chapel Street and away from her.

Now I have always been an asthmatic and needed to take a Ventolin everywhere I went. Tonight I had left my asthma pump in Bettina's handbag and it was important that I get it back. Recently I had experienced an asthma attack in the middle of the night, I was short of breath for six straight hours. It wasn't pleasant, just sitting there struggling for breath till the chemist opened. The attacks where never serious enough to warrant hospital, but they weren't fun either.

I yelled at her on the phone to leave it out the front of her apartment, but no, Bettina wanted to have a bit of fun with my neediness. Bettina said she couldn't make it there, so I yelled at her to meet me in Chapel Street, near Revolver. Bettina was enjoying having the upper hand, it was a case of 'You need me now, you dirty fuck boy', which in hindsight I completely understand, but at the time I was distraught with rage. How dare she show me that level of disrespect? The drugs were coursing through my body and I remember feeling like the Incredible Hulk.

Bettina was in the passenger seat and her friend was driving, when I saw their car, something in me just clicked. I ran past two police officers arresting someone to jump from the gutter straight onto the bonnet of the car. It was like some crazy crouching tiger moment, I produced one kick and knocked the whole windscreen into their car. I was thinking, 'Great now I have your undivided attention.' I punched the passenger side window out and told her to leave me the fuck alone.

People came from everywhere to smash into me, a team of blokes pinned me on the ground and started kicking the shit out of me. I lay there in complete peace, it was a weird feeling. There was a massive emotional shift for me the second I released my rage and even though my head was getting punched into the concrete like a speed ball, I felt happy. Thank God for the police, they rushed over and stopped the angry mob from lynching me. There were a couple of guys assisting Bettina, who was playing the damsel in distress. These meatheads took one look at her and decided I should burn on the cross for treating such an attractive woman this way. They were exuberant with my punishment.

The coppers were fantastic, they bundled me into the back of the sedan away from the marauding mob. For a minute I sat there in peace, thinking Bettina would never bother me again—wrong, wrong. She was obsessed with this lunatic, obsessed. Even she used to admit that, when I asked her why she couldn't leave me alone.

After sitting in the police car for a little bit, I began thinking—

when I get back to the cells the police are going to search me—if they search me they are going to find a bunch of shit in a cigarette packet that isn't legal. So I began breathing heavily in the back of the car to fog up the windows. It worked, with the windows fogged I set about moving the cigarette packet from my jacket pocket and into my jocks, with handcuffs on and my hands behind my back. Anyone that has been handcuffed will know the police put them on so hard they cut into your wrists. But I was committed and though the metal cut into my skin, I managed to get it done. It was an extremely painful experience, but I would rather deal with that pain than have the police come back to my house and see what I had there.

When I got to the cells, they searched me with my clothes on and I managed to keep the packet beneath my balls. I was very honest in the interview and when the officers asked why I did it, I explained that I was an idiot. Bettina and her friend were in another interview room. I explained to the officers they were wasting their time interviewing them. I knew they wouldn't make a statement against me. The officers came in and confirmed what I had told them. The police charged me with reckless criminal damage and told me to sort out the bill for the windscreen and passenger window with the owner. Then I spent a few hours sleeping in the cells of the Prahran police station.

It was still dark when the coppers let me out. I walked home cold and in the dark but I wasn't going to be here much longer. I had a counter meal at the Orrong Hotel on the Sunday night and as I sat there by myself, battered and bruised, Carlos rang me to say he heard about what had happened and wanted to make sure I was okay. I was okay, I was better than I had been for a long time, there was a clearing of energy that evening and I knew some change was at hand.

The courts ended up giving me a special order banning me from going within five hundred metres of Chapel Street for two years. Barred from Chapel Street, damn.

HARD TIMES

'Life has many ways of testing a person's will, either by having nothing happen at all or by having everything happen at once.'
— Paulo Coelho

Even after the situation out the front of Revolver, my never-say-die ex-missus Bettina was still trying to come over. She wouldn't, or couldn't stop, it was complete madness. I decided I needed to take some drastic action, I needed to send back all her belongings.

Bettina had moved out of home at fifteen, I was asked to leave home at twenty. I moved straight in with Bettina and all her stuff. My clothes were the only things I took with me, everything else at my apartment was hers. In order to end this relationship, I needed to send back all her things and go without for a while. Things were a lot tighter financially now that I had decided to stop most of my illegal activities. I was willing to go without the basic necessities in life, if it meant this relationship between Bettina and myself were done.

As the removalists took the last of Bettina's things back to her parents' place, I could not believe how empty the apartment was.

All that was left was a wooden deck chair, a radio, two dumbbells, a doona, a pillow and my clothes. Nothing else; no fridge, no mattress, nothing at all. Now it was time for me to live like a monk, this spartan existence was going to be my reality for a time.

As soon as Bettina's belongings arrived at her parents' place, she realised what this meant and headed over to my apartment to try and make amends. When she arrived and saw the stark reality of how I was living she became upset.

Living like this was a challenge at the beginning, the toughest part for me was sleeping on the floor with only a pillow and a doona. Later on I found out this sleeping arrangement was excellent for my back; the problem was lying down for an evening on the carpeted floor. It took a hell of a lot of getting used to. In the morning I would wake up, go for a run and do some weights and grab something to eat. Then I would head home and sit on my wooden chair and listen to Gold FM. It was around this time that I changed my phone number again.

If I was going to make a go of changing my life, cutting ties with existing associations was probably the most important decision I had to make. Going from such an active and time consuming social life to absolutely nothing was extremely confronting. Just because you cease communication with old acquaintances doesn't mean you immediately forget everything. In fact, now that my mind and body had time to process what I had just been through, I slipped into overdrive and began to feel as if I was going mad.

It was interesting because on some spiritual level I felt that how I was living was something I needed to do. There were many offers of furniture but I refused. My soul was telling me that I needed to do this. It was like a cleanse. I needed to hit the reset button.

When I began to process what had happened over the last few years, I slipped into deep self-reflection. Some may call this depression but I saw it as a kind of active meditation. Previously my life was an out of control express train, moving so fast that I missed key moments and overlooked people. Now was my opportunity to contemplate and decode the hidden meanings and life lessons. So even though the content matter I was sifting through was dark and difficult, I had a sense of purpose. This was work I needed to do, in order to get back to any sort of normality. The problem was that as I started reliving some of the key moments of what had been my life, I began to question whether I was ever going to be able to function at a reasonable level again.

The most interesting part for me was how the mind and soul cope with the little to no human interaction. This began primarily because I had lost faith and trust in myself and by that admission, in other people. I decided originally that I would keep to myself and see where that journey took me.

It was an amazing ride. I found exploring the human mind to be like driving a car. There were the dark tunnels, dead-end streets, highways, freeways and intersections. What I found was that there was no problem moving through any of these areas, as long as you keep moving. Indecision or procrastination can have you stall or break down in a dark tunnel. This can be challenging—say you stall in a dead end street, it can be tricky to back yourself out of that. I went on a long journey of self-exploration and over a long period of time I discovered that I was as happy with my own company as anyone else's.

My focus now shifted to repairing the damage I had caused with my family; my brother Paul was the key to healing these wounds. Paul Hibiscus Lawrence Harding had never given up on me, we stayed in contact throughout my whole time away from everyone. Being the youngest, he must have heard some terrible things about me. Taking into consideration that I was a trailblazing hooligan, my family would have had a hard time dealing with my actions. Even through this mess Pablo kept in contact; he would tell me what was going on at home and ask me to buy him porno movies. Then out of the blue he rang me up and asked to come to my place and hang out. It's funny the way life works. There was a feeling that I had done enough work to be able to associate with straight heads again. Then right on cue, my brother rings wanting to hang out. It had been quite some time since I had socialised, so although I was apprehensive, the thought of seeing my little brother and having a counter meal was exciting.

The Orrong Hotel had become my local pub, it was fascinating that after all the nightclubbing and discotheques, here I was back with your average everyday punters at the local. My new routine consisted of getting to the Orrong at around 11am, have a couple of beers, bets and a counter meal, then head home. When I was home I would punch a few cones and have an afternoon nap. I would be back up at the pub around 5pm for the evening meal. I met some really nice people up there and the owners at the time were fantastic with me. They had years of experience in this trade and probably read my situation blind. The wife was lovely to me, she showed me a lot of kindness during this period. My brother was coming over to my apartment a lot and then I began to go back home for dinner.

THE KING AND I, ST. KILDA

'Fear comes from uncertainty; we can eliminate the fear within us when we know ourselves better.'
— Bruce Lee

In St. Kilda there is an old blue mansion near the corner of Nepean Highway and Alma Road, not dissimilar to the Gatwick on Fitzroy Street. The Blue House is like a magnet for a certain subculture. The house is a twenty-four-hour, seven-day-a-week hub for the criminally insane. It's all about business and making money to purchase drugs. Street-level sex workers sublet rooms from the inhabitants of the Blue House for a night. This lets them ply their trade, which brings sexually frustrated husbands and kinky straight men into the fray. Sometimes the sex workers will organise the homeless or regulars at the Blue House to rob one of their clients, knowing damn well the client can't do anything about it.

The mentally challenged and homeless congregate here and work together with the occupants to devise ways of making money to score drugs. Drugs are the glue that brings all the different groups together. Everyone is looking to escape their reality in one way or another.

Heroin and ice addicts use the house as a shooting gallery, they forge friendships with the people who live there so they can give them a taste of whatever they are holding in order to enjoy their high within the confines of a safe place. Some stay awake for days on end, fall into zombie-like states, become paranoid and talk shorthand gibberish. One wrong look at this stage can result in extreme violence because, deep down, everyone is scared. Mid-level drug dealers supply trusted members of the house with heroin, ice, marijuana and prescription drugs. They give contraband to the occupants on credit knowing damn well they have a captive audience and don't have anywhere to go. The dealers make good money off a place like this, profiting from another human's demise.

Men and women who have completed lengthy prison sentences, anywhere from ten to twenty year stretches, flock together at the Blue House with like-minded people that speak and understand their language and way of thinking. Usually they are murderers, old-fashioned bank robbers and lifetime recidivists that do not know anything other than the four walls of a jail. They find comfort with people cut from the same cloth.

My lifestyle has allowed me the pleasure of being able to integrate and socialise in plenty of different socio-economic circles. When I met the King, I couldn't help but notice how he treated everyone with the same level of respect. The King never judged anyone and from the moment I met him, I felt a deep connection with him. The King, and I call him this because of the way he looks after people, is an underworld legend. He ran a lot of the casinos before the Crown Casino opened up in Melbourne. He has survived underworld wars, when others have perished. The King was originally a big player on the Waterfront in the 70s and is the best poker player I have had the pleasure of losing money to. Out of respect for the great man, I won't go into too much detail about his life, other than he was born and raised in Collingwood and follows the mighty Magpies. The King is an extremely private man and rarely lets his emotions dictate his course of action. I was lucky to even get a seat at his table—it's what you call a closed school. It's made up of old-school knockabouts, crooks and gangsters. The King is the ringleader and this is clear by the amount of respect everyone treats him with. The experience and knowledge you gain from sitting down and eating with men like this is invaluable, they constantly attack each other like sharks. Its entertaining stuff.

To the King, it didn't matter if you were the Prince of Penzance or if you had an addiction to heroin and only three teeth. The King always treated everyone the same. It was a beautiful standard for me to aspire to. At the club where all the heads play poker, it is nothing to see some very serious people there. The best is when people come in, down on their luck and the King will give them a job or something to do, so they can earn a little bit of scratch to go on with. The King will get them to sweep up the driveway, wash his car or clean the dishes. It would be easy to fob these people off because of what they look like. Not the King, in another life this man would have been a great leader. I felt a magnetic pull to him. I am selective about who my wife and children meet and they have met the King.

I was first introduced to this Blue House by a St. Kilda sex worker I knew. Every year around Christmas, there is a choof drought in Melbourne and it can be tricky to purchase any if you don't know anyone. My gang was struggling to get some so I decided to drive to St. Kilda and see who was working—the street girls always knew who was holding gear.

Sarah, a girl I had known for a while, was on the streets and I pulled over, jumped out of the car and had a smoke with her. We discussed life and how she was going, before I asked her if she could direct me in the way of some choof. Sarah said that was no problem, she would take me to meet Stumpy up in the magical Blue House.

When we arrived I felt some apprehension about walking into the unknown. The monstrous period house we pulled up at was a house I had driven past many times before. Sarah and I walked up the steel staircase to the second level and then she opened the door to a corridor of bedrooms. I was surprised to see a massive blood stained wall, this place was the sort you hear about, but never get to see. This was the end of the line, one step before being on the streets.

The smell of piss and desperation overwhelmed me. Sarah introduced me to Stumpy and it struck me like a thunderbolt: I was going to learn some incredible life stories of the people from the magical Blue House in east St. Kilda.

Stumpy was a short, overweight man with an 80s permed mullet. He wore old track pants, Dunlop KT'26 runners and an open leather vest, so that all his chest hair was showing. He talked in a machine gun fashion, very much like Warwick Capper. My new friend Stumpy was definitely a few things, but simple wasn't one of them. 'Survivor' is the word that comes to mind when I think of him.

I hung around and chatted with Stumpy for a little bit, he had an entertaining way. Stumpy was sure of himself and explained to me that he needed to smash this dog, as in, a person, who had come sniffing around his joint the other night. Then he gestured to the blood stained wall with his hand and I nodded to acknowledge what he had said. He ended up pouring out his whole life story and I listened to him. We ended up becoming friends until he mysteriously had to leave and then I met the next bloke who moved in, he introduced me to the whole village down there.

There was one bloke who lived there who watched the horse racing all day long in a smoke-filled room. This bloke had female pornographic pictures all over his place. Every inch of the walls and ceiling was covered with hardcore erotica. It was insane to see him in this room covered in stick books. He probably just whacked himself off all day, watched the horse races and smoked cigarettes.

There was another bloke there who tried to re-condition the engine of his car while he was flying on ice, he talked like Ben Johnson ran. Right off his head, this bloke clearly had no idea what he was doing. It was a clapped out old VS Commodore sedan and he had ripped the seats out, taken off water pumps, unwired whatever he could and laid out everything neatly on the lawn. He charged over to me and tried to explain what he was doing and I was fairly interested. The only problem was that he was flying so hard from taking ice, his words weren't making any sense. The gentleman thought he was speaking perfect English and all of his ideas were wonderful. What I heard was passionate gibberish. It's important to be supportive of an ice-head and their wacky ideas, that way, they don't feel threatened. I nodded my head at the times I thought appropriate in this unconventional conversation. I passed with flying colours, the ice-head now trusted me completely and explained his whole life while I listened and nodded without understanding a word.

I couldn't help but think back to another encounter that has stayed with me. I had been working in the city one evening and was walking down an alleyway near Degraves Street when I found a short, middle-aged woman furiously tearing through the garbage. Initially my senses told me that something was amiss, but I gave her the benefit of the doubt. This poor woman had heard and seen me get closer to her, but the commitment to her task never waned. The woman was ripping and pulling waste apart so intensely I wondered if she may have lost an expensive ring or family heirloom. My common sense told me that someone with an expensive ring probably wouldn't be in a garbage bin, in a dark alley in the CBD at 4am.

I decided to say hello and see if she needed my help. She acknowledged my greeting and explained that she just needed to look through rubbish. I nodded and went about my business, it wasn't until I had another good look at her did I realise I knew this woman from the methadone clinic in Ormond. I used to say hello and chat with all the addicts that went in and out of that clinic, in fact I became familiar with most of them. This woman had lots of tattoos and looked a lot healthier then the last time I saw her. She always seemed friendly and I could tell she had lived a tough life. I feel an overwhelming sense of compassion for people that have walked the hard road. Any time I have taken the opportunity to listen to the story of a battler, I have gained a real sense of how their situation evolved. This process is rewarding for a curious person like myself.

It's far too easy to label or judge another human being who is struggling with addiction. It's not until you see someone so incredibly focused on a task that can be best described as unhygienic, do you realise how strong the addiction can be. I took a good look at the facial expressions of this lady and I noticed her jaw was clenched tight and her face was taught. At this point her perception of reality was so far removed from normality, a warm bed in the hospital was probably the safest place to wear this beast of a drug into submission.

I saw this chance meeting with the waste-sorting woman as a metaphor for my life during those drug-fuelled years. Here she was off her head, going hell-for-leather trying to achieve something. Her intentions came from the right place, she needed to feel like she was getting something done while she was using drugs. In my situation there was no difference: I was running around town like a maniac, doing my best to get ahead. There was that same need to feel as though my life had meaning.

I guess through my associations with the King and my father, I have always found a way to humanise the people I have met who find themselves in less fortunate situations.

THE DARK ART OF VIOLENCE

'By the pricking of my thumbs, something wicked this way comes.'
— William Shakespeare

Violence is an art form and the ability to inflict pain on someone precisely the way you want to, is a tremendous brush stroke. It's only when the aggressor gets carried away with his work do things get ugly; this usually happens when the aggressor is a bloodthirsty sociopath or high on drugs.

There were many times in my old profession when I saw people get caught up trying to be a heavy. They would start dressing and behaving like a gangster version of themselves. When it came down to the nitty gritty, these pretenders didn't have the minerals. It would always be a case of coming in with a gang of people behind them. Sometimes these sorts of characters would tool up with a shooter or they would get high on drugs. All three things are a recipe for jail time or someone getting hurt.

Take scenario one: An insecure wannabe who is owed money will bring in some backup. Now you have a little crew of amateurs looking to inflict pain on the guy who owes money. A bloke in this situation will do anything to avoid an ass-whipping, including lying or going to the police. So either way the wannabe gangsters are going to have to take action. I know a few blokes who have done jail time because the target has run to the police out of fear. The wannabes have over-played their hand and have come in too heavy, then the terrified target has opened up to the jacks like a tin of tuna. The police get the target to arrange a meeting to which they are privy, then when the wannabes roll up, ready to keep it gangster, the cuffs are on and charges of threatening to kill get thrown around the magistrate's court.

The next scenario is not much better. Coming in locked and loaded with a gun is a dangerous proposition for all parties involved. This includes the people who have sold the gun to the wannabe tough guy. I have seen it time and time again, the minute you put a shooter in the hand of an inexperienced guy, it's an instantaneous parody of Rambo, you can tell by the way they hold it. Their personality changes and the bravado begins, they get around with a certain swagger and walk and talk like they are invincible. All because they have some steel with them. Often the wannabe's gun will never see the light of day, it stays in a cupboard until they have a few drinks, then they get it out and wave it around a bit to impress people at their house. It's when a situation gets heavy and the would-be gangster decides to bring the heat along with him, do you have a problem. Say he pulls it out and the target shits himself and tries to attack the guy with the gun. He has to shoot now and if he doesn't, the target will try to take it off him or do anything to eliminate the chance of getting shot. The tough guy can't call a timeout and say 'I was only joking; it was all for show. I don't really want to kill you.' This is how a lot of people get shot or killed—inexperienced males on a power trip.

Last but not least is the most common scenario: young wannabes needing to take drugs to give them the edge they lack to complete an act of violence. You see it on the news, in the paper and on the radio. Youngsters playing the game. It's a sad situation. I am beginning to hear some worrying things about the youth of today, linking them with home invasions and carjackings. A bunch of young blokes get offered some cash to do a home invasion, usually to retrieve some pride and money for an older, experienced crook who is too smart to do the dirty work himself. The young, inexperienced crew get high on ice before the act because they are scared shitless. In they go, undoubtedly one of the occupants will staunch up to the crew of young kids and trouble will ensue. Instead of doing what needs to be done to contain the situation, the crew go overboard and the situation escalates. Grievous bodily harm or manslaughter charges are laid and a group of young lives are ruined, all because of one silly act. They struggle to get jobs for the rest of their lives and the downwards spiral continues.

There is an art to violence. I was damn good at it; I used the underlying threat of violence to gain the upper hand. A lot of the time I dealt with people who knew what I was willing to do and this was a massive hand to be able to play. If someone knows you are ready to take things to the next level, they are more than likely to do exactly what you want. It was rare that I had to actually be violent—more often than not just turning up unexpectedly was enough to rattle a cage. The psychology of fear is what I got off on. I started to practise different techniques relating to the person or situation and became a well-rounded judge of character. If you can read the play before the fact, does the target stand a chance?

What I found out towards the end of my career was I sympathised with the target's situation and, let's face it, you can't have a heavy commiserating with the mark, can you? I would end up putting people on payment plans and all sorts of deals to help them wriggle out of situations they would normally expect pain from. I became a real soft touch and this is when I knew I needed to get out of that game. I would sit down with these people and begin to listen and understand their stories and lives. Once you put the time in, they become human. It was through this I realised I wanted to help people. My journey in life had taken me all the way through the darkness and back towards the light. My experience helped me understand the harrowing life lessons some of these characters have been through and it is now my role to do all I can to serve humanity.

Someone upstairs decided to let me off the hook, there were many occasions where things got really close and I could have been one of the statistics. But that wasn't my journey, my position now comes from a place of kindness, compassion, empathy and understanding. After all I have been a part of, there can be no judgement from me. Any of my clients from that side of the tracks, can sniff out judgement a mile away and that's the last thing they want when they are trying to become strong. My role is to help people believe in themselves and show them there is always an opportunity to walk towards the light.

HOUSE OF CARDS

'There's nothing wrong with enjoying looking at the surface of the ocean itself, except that when you finally see what goes on underwater, you realize that you've been missing the whole point of the ocean.'
— Dave Barry

This is what I have learned about the underworld: people from this world don't refer to it as the underworld, it's the way of life they have always known. There are separate rules and regulations for that world where crossing the police and going to jail is all part of the process. In this world people from 'normal society' are referred to as 'straighties' or 'square heads', nine-to-five type operators that punch in at work, pay taxes and generally do the righty.

Normally these two worlds don't have much to do with each other, but every now and again the underworld will have a cleanout or, as the media call it, 'a gangland war'. David Hookes the cricketer who was felled with one punch in St. Kilda and sadly passed away, is the perfect example of what I am talking about. He would tell anyone that would listen how he had a beer next to Graham 'the

Munster' Kinniburgh at the Orrong Hotel.

Melbourne, and the rest of the world, loves true crime. It's grotesque and ugly but so hard to look away from. No doubt somewhere along the journey you would have crossed paths with someone from this world and you will have a tale. If you personally don't, you will know someone that has. Melbourne, in particular, has a love of criminality; it's almost as if we are proud of our criminal background: from the convicts who settled in this country to Ned Kelly, the outlaw bushranger who refused to yield to the powers that be. We also have Squizzy Taylor, Chopper Read and Mighty Mick Gatto. Our thirst for crime stories is insatiable.

High society and criminality are a lot more closely aligned than many people think—big business people keep gangsters in their pocket right next to their Mont Blanc pens. When push comes to shove and you're dealing with millions of dollars or massive contracts, the serious movers and shakers of the underworld are the ones who can get things done. Their propensity for violence and willingness to go to the next level is something high society likes to call on when a situation doesn't go the way they planned. This was brought to my attention when I sat in the front row at the kickboxing as a personal guest of a serious corporate player.

The kickboxing and boxing is a haven for underworld activity. The crooks show up in droves with all the pomp and ceremony at these events. Some of the main guests I was sitting with were the high society from the top end of town: CEOs of major companies, politicians, powerbrokers, socialites regularly seen in the newspapers, knockabouts, and gangsters. I can assure you that when the top end of town gets together for a dinner party, they will be dropping all sorts of names to their guests and the guests will be hanging off their every word with morbid fascination. You know why? Because they're no different to anyone else, they are intrigued by what lurks in the shadows and goes bump in the night.

Many of the big players of the underworld enjoy the notoriety of being in bed with straighties from the big leagues. Just like regular society, the criminal world has many different classes and the top criminals that you will never hear about and will never see the inside of a jail cell have learned very quickly: if you run things like a business and insulate yourself from any collateral damage, chances are that you are going to live a very comfortable life. Now, where do you think this notion started from, running a criminal enterprise like a business? Corporate players in bed with the upper echelons of the criminal world. They all use each other for the same reasons: to get ahead and make money.

The people you read about in the papers blowing each others heads off in the back blocks of an industrial wasteland don't get anywhere near the top dogs. They are as dispensable as a soiled nappy and even though you will get a hundred and one blokes in dark suits wearing sunglasses and gold chains at their funeral, they're nowhere near the boss. The papers will pump it up as a gangland slaying to sell papers, but the truth is the papers have no fucking idea what is going on, just like the poor bugger in the box they are lowering into the ground.

Up the top, there are all sorts of dummy companies used to launder money, accountants, lawyers and financial advisors. Long gone are the days of cold hard cash in safes and under mattresses, the top dogs of the underworld have evolved with the times. When there is so much money involved in the drug industry—and it is an industry—it's only natural the rewards of being on top of a drug empire evolve as well.

What I mean by this is that you have your basic run-of-the-mill crook who will find a way to earn good money, but the money doesn't last forever. So rather than making hay while the sun shines, they will piss it up against the wall with a brand new Mercedes, fancy restaurants, spunky ladies and drugs. Then they end up broke and reminisce about the good old days at the local pub while waiting for their next Centrelink payment.

On the other hand, criminals with a want for a better life put away every cent of the earn and they keep quiet about their progress. As soon as the writing is on the wall and the rort dries up, bang, they bankroll their cash with a legitimate business partner and sound financial advice. Hey presto, you have the makings of a successful business enterprise. I know a few blokes who have started this way and you would be shocked at what businesses were originally funded by the darker side of life. These people own successful bars overseas, holiday houses, have their children go to the best private schools and now run with the people from the top end of town.

In days gone past criminals were some solid units first and foremost, strong characters that didn't buckle inside a police station and this was when the police were as violent as the crooks they were chasing. Some of the older Painters and Dockers I catch up with from an era past have told me horror stories of what they endured at the hands of the police. Brutal bashings by men hell-bent on enforcing the law and their own form of justice. These days the police have to punch the criminals to shut them up in a police station, they are that willing to give up their associates. It's disgusting. There was a time when you needed a skillset to be involved in any criminal activity as a safe-cracker, armed robber, fraud or importer and you had to have the respect of the hierarchy to get a start. These days allegiances change like the wind and drugs dictate where loyalties lie.

Any time I have been in a police station for an interview, I asked more questions than the police did. Call me old-fashioned but no one has done a day's jail because of me and I'm proud of that. The golden rule of the underworld is not to give people up, but that theory has evolved as well. These days there are all sorts of ways people put other blokes in and wriggle out of jail time. Too many technicalities and far too much of a grey area for my liking. I got into this with the grandiose idea that criminals were rock solid and despised the thought of lowering their colours with a statement to the cops. I could not have been more wrong about that. As I mentioned before, massive empires have been brought down by snivelling junkies privy to information they really should not have known about.

This brings me to another rule of the underworld; don't tell anyone what you are doing. This rule was hilarious since a large portion of players of the underworld are, by nature, the biggest gigs going around. I found it to be a showy affair, full of people who were keen to take centre stage and make it all about themselves.

This is the sole reason I tried to avoid working with people, always trying to do things by myself. This way if I was brought undone it was because of my own doing and I could live with that. Obviously, there were times when you can't help but work with different crews, the thing is you can limit any information you tell the people you are working with. One gang I was involved with at different times said; 'You're like a fucking fox, you hide in your little hole and you pop up when it's time to do something, then you're gone again.' No one knew where I lived and I regularly changed my phone number and hardly ever drove my own car. The fact that I was never caught may have something to do with this.

In the scheme of things, I was very small. But I didn't get pinched for anything I was involved in. For me, it was always about risk and reward—if the risk outweighed the reward it was a no-brainer. My passion was consuming drugs first and foremost; I loved getting off my head and enjoying the high. I didn't fancy paying for any of it and working an honest job wasn't going to suffice—my intake was beyond the average wage. So illegal activity was the only option. I made plenty of mistakes, but I always limited the damage by making reasonably sound decisions first and I did this by using the skills that have served me so well over the years and continue to do so. My instinct, intuition and exceptional memory, the internal computer inside my head, have been a blessing. So many times during the journey I didn't do things because it didn't feel right and my instincts proved to be correct.

I have read that Yasser Arafat had this innate ability to feel when things were about to go wrong and would leave wherever he was. Sure enough, there would be a hit squad on their way and had he stayed he would have been brown bread.

I am also a tremendous listener and I used this skill to my advantage in that world. By listening to people's problems, I learned from their mistakes and this gave me a crash course in what not to do, coupled with my memory retention I was able to recall information at the right times to keep me out of harm's way.

More than anything I was an opportunist, if there was an opportunity to earn and that opportunity fell within my capability, then I would seize it.

If you have ever had the intestinal fortitude that has allowed you to ride one of those terrifying roller coasters that scare the fuck out of everyone on the ride, then you have an idea of the emotions involved in dealing with the underworld. Now imagine that ride lasting five long years. Five years of not knowing whether the police will smash down your door while you're asleep or some rooster is looking to take a scalp and annihilate you. When I do something I do it with my whole heart and when I commit with such ferocity it's always going to be an emotional journey. I have definitely left pieces of myself all over this magnificent town and I know this because wherever I go in Melbourne I have a story and that makes me smile. When I began the road less travelled I had an end date and I stuck to that, my journey was about looking behind the curtains and seeing what was backstage. I had no doubt in my mind that I could grow and succeed. I figured if I could make a fist of life and survive in the unknown behind the curtains, then I could survive and prosper anywhere. It just so happened that I was right on both accounts, I gambled on myself and ended up with experiences that have proven to serve me in the most astonishing ways. There were no limiting thought patterns, I grabbed life and throttled it by the neck soaking up everything I could from it and enjoyed the ride.

You can take me to any city in the world and put me in the roughest and most volatile places, I know how to handle myself so that thought is an inspiring one.

OUT OF SIGHT, OUT OF MIND

'I know where I'm going and I know the truth. I don't have to be what you want me to be. I'm free to be what I want.'
— Muhammad Ali

When I was about twenty-five I decided that it was time to move away. I took myself up the coast and over the border to find some peace and quiet. The local football club welcomed me with open arms—they saw a key position player because of my height. I hadn't done anything physical in about four years, the closest thing I had done to training involved the dance floor at 161 or flogging someone that owed money. The football club organised a job for me and I started to find my way up there. Buck moved in with me and we enjoyed the bachelor lifestyle. Every Sunday afternoon we would take a few beers to a rock-fishing spot I had found where we relaxed and caught fish. Well I did anyway, Buck seemed to set a lot of hooks into rocks, then he would fight the rock, which he claimed to be a massive grouper. Massive rock grouper, yeah right.

I began to eat a lot of pasta and drink a lot of beer. My frame when I moved up the coast was around 70kg, I looked boned out and gaunt, my eyes told the story of where I had been. By the end of the first year, I had put on 15kg and was looking healthier. Things were coming together and I became part of the town, it was a special place being up on the coast. To go from not being in the salt water for years, to waking up with it out the front of your bedroom was a big change. I started swimming and we spent a bit of time spearfishing and surfing.

It was a simpler life, things moved slowly up there and that suited me just fine. My frame of mind was more grounded and the town was full of interesting characters.

People are more authentic in the country. With such a huge population in the city, you can afford to have a few different social circles. If you happen to be one of those people who find it hard to do the right thing, you can hide a bit and get away with it. In the country you can't hide, you have to be a nice person or you are going to be branded a wanker.

The footy club had set me up and all they wanted from me was to hold down the two hardest positions on the ground: ruckman changing at centre half-forward. They were positions that required me to be physical and I had the body of an emaciated drug addict.

I didn't know how I was going to play football, this wasn't in the stars at all. The club had done the right thing by me, so I needed to find a way to get it done. I had a few games where I dominated and that was fun. I loved being around solid people, it allowed me to start trusting again and the after-match functions were enjoyable.

I first noticed Buck on the football field throwing up on the wing. He had come up the coast to get away from some minor dramas down at his home and he ended up playing football with our local side. He hadn't played for years and had been in England enjoying the nightlife a little too much. The footy match had proved to be a winner, he received the bottomless mug for one of the best afield.

Buckso is a country boy through and through, an honest and

loyal mate with a heart of gold. Buck has a lot of tattoos, he speaks with a laid back country drawl and swears all the time. He says things like, 'That steak was tender as fuck,' he calls alcohol 'piss' and toilet paper 'bum fodder'. He is six foot with a wiry frame and boy does he love a blue. I met him at the local footy one day, when I was playing interstate and we have been close mates ever since. The thing I loved most about Buck is that he fancies himself as quite the bushman.

Buck happened to end up at my house blind drunk and slurring incoherently, so I grabbed a teaspoon of speed and popped it into his mouth while it was open. Buck recognised the taste instantly, then started giggling. Buck laughs like Cletus the Slack-Jawed Yokel from *The Simpsons*. We went back to the footy club and had a great night; Buck got up on stage and started telling little Johnny gags. Then he started hanging shit on some of the senior players, it was priceless stuff. I liked him immediately.

Then one Monday I pulled a sickie and drove home to find him parked at the beach staring into the sunset. I told him to come and have a beer. Buck commented that it was 8.30am. So I told him to come and have a cup of tea, then a beer. Turns out the bloke Buck was staying with from the footy club was engaged and having a kid with this girl, Stacker. Stacker and Buck had a one-night stand many years ago. So the bloke got jealous of Buck and he had to move out, hence he was down at the beach pondering what to do next. He couldn't go back home at that time; his hands were tied.

I asked him if he wanted to move in on the spot. I hadn't lived with anyone in a long time but I knew that I could trust and be honest with him. From that moment I'd gained a lifelong friend. We have been through so much together and are still close mates; he was one of the groomsmen at my wedding.

Buck is one of the staunchest and most loyal of friends. Buck is handy in a tight situation. He isn't scared to tell anyone what he thinks and I love that trait in a person.

There were times on the coast when the work dried up and I was forced to come back to Melbourne and do a few things to pay the bills. It wasn't a nice feeling; my old life would continue to reappear, constantly reminding me of what I had once been. Being back in Melbourne I would bump into different people and they would ask if I was back—I certainly was not back.

While I was up there some debt collectors from the bank chased me up regarding a personal loan I had taken out years ago. There were some other bits and pieces hanging over me, like nearly $10k worth of speeding and parking fines. All my bad debts had come home to roost. I consulted a professional and decided to go bankrupt. It was ironic being chased for a debt, I thoroughly enjoyed the process. Wayne was the bloke putting the squeeze on me. He told me how I was going to be blacklisted and this would last forever. I wouldn't be able to get a home loan or anything. This mark against my name would have repercussions and I believed him. He was in charge of scaring me into paying it back. These conversations were so much fun and I learned a lot about how easy it is to get the final figure down.

For example, say the final figure of all my debts was $50k, Wayne would ask for it. I would tell him I didn't have it; he would make out like there was a dark cloud of impending doom hanging over my head and I was supposed to buckle and pay the money back. I wanted to know what happened if I didn't pay, so Wonderful Wayne offered me a payment plan to which I declined. Then Wayne asked me what I could afford. How good was this bloke? Wonderful Wayne asked if I could afford $35k, I said no. Then Wonderful Wayne offered $20k, I said no. Wonderful Wayne cracked the shits and brought up the blacklist again. This experience showed me that debt collecting without threat of physical violence was more of a conversation than a collection. Wonderful Wayne wasn't collecting a damn thing from me. I had done some research myself and bankruptcy was a much better option—Wonderful Wayne certainly didn't want me to know about this. When I alerted him of the choice I had made, it snatched the confidence from deep inside him and he realised it was checkmate. See you later pal.

It was an amazing lifestyle up there; the fishing was on another level. Some of the locals took me to remote spots that involved long 4WD trips to get there. I was in heaven: fishing, football and a community feel that allowed me to find the person I had lost touch with a long time ago. The locals gave me the chance to integrate into their way of life and it was a relaxing way to live. The bullshit doesn't exist with country folk and that was reassuring. I found my faith in people up on the coast and I will be forever thankful to them.

My new home up the coast was exactly that, home. I told Carlos to tell everyone that I was in jail on some gun charges interstate. The perfect throw-off. The only thing that was missing up on the coast were women, they were non-existent. I was now sober and functioning well, women were the one non-negotiable I couldn't go without. The style with which I had become used to came to a screeching halt. I tried the local RSL, there was nothing cooking at all, nothing, not a girl my age in sight. This was always going to be a problem, I wasn't a monk anymore. My body was in good shape and my mind was clear. It was a shame. But obviously I wasn't meant to settle up there yet.

After two years, Melbourne started beckoning me home. The need to be back around my family was clear. Whenever they would come up to my place on the coast and it came time for them to leave, I was sad to see them go. I wanted to go with them. That is how I knew it wasn't my home.

The work began to dry up and the romantic situation was not getting any better. Buck and I organised a removalist to come and pick up our stuff and take it back to Melbourne. We said goodbye to all our friends and thanked them for everything they had done for the both of us. It was a sad moment and even now I get upset thinking back on it.

So many solid memories up there. I'll never forget the place and the people. I arrived a 70kg drug addicted mess, with some serious trust issues. I left with a brand new version of myself, close to 90kg and I had a renewed faith in life.

HOMECOMING

'Being a drug addict isn't nearly as bad as being sober and loving a drug addict. Whether it's a family member, spouse or friend. Nothing will screw you up more than being associated with a drug addict. You can't save them but they can sure as hell destroy you—and they will.'
— unknown

Dad had organised a place for me to rent under his name. Under the rules of bankruptcy you can't rent a house in your name. It was a modest house that suited our purposes. From the moment I got back it was my worst nightmare. One big party.

My fears were realised when lots of people from my past wanted to catch up and make up for lost time. I was apprehensive about falling back into old habits but the partying and women were impossible to say no to. What started as catching up, turned into a year long bender. I was pinched driving intoxicated and lost my licence for twenty months. This was a major setback and the catalyst for some important portions of my life being spent drinking at pubs. I was still trying to do the right thing and I obtained gainful employment at a pre-fabrication truss and framing plant, it paid $600 a week. Not much of an incentive to work is it? Getting to work involved waking at 4:30am and walking 2km from my house to get to the station, training it for thirty minutes, then catching a bus or walking another 2km to get to the warehouse. Even though it was a pain in the arse, I continued to slog away at this dead end job.

During this time an old friend of mine caught up with me and mentioned he had these ecstasy pills that he needed help moving. There was some massive coin involved and the opportunity was too good to refuse. It didn't take long to get the pills moving and it was lovely to have some real money coming in. The funniest thing is I continued to work at the plant out of some sense of wanting to be legitimate. $600 dollars a week puts enormous pressure on the budget and leaves you feeling undervalued. Around this time a big gang of us went out to Revolver. I was supposed to be working that weekend. As I dropped my eighth pill on the Sunday morning at Revs, I began to get a strange problem with my eyes. I couldn't see myself going to work at all that weekend, in fact I couldn't see a damn thing. Those pills were insanely strong and I was struggling to stand.

On the Monday I was called to a meeting at the office and was fired. I completely understood where the manager was coming from and I apologised for my indiscretion. I was bloody happy to be out of that joint, there is nothing more deflating in life than being underpaid or undervalued. It's soul destroying.

Here I was back in business with plenty of cash and time on my hands. I used to call this line of work, 'living off the land'; it helped me feel better about doing what I knew was morally wrong. Even though I was socialising with undesirable characters again, my focus was on finding employment and getting my life together. My Dad rang me one day and I explained to him where I was in my life and he understood my situation. Dad didn't agree with all my illegal activity and it came to a head one evening.

Dad and Mum were walking the dogs and I was heading to the local pub with Sminger, we had just been at his place—I was using it as a safe house. My parents caught me off guard and the whole situation looked dodgy, even though Sminger was not involved in this business at all. Dad was concerned and rang me later that evening, he picked me up from the pub and we drove to a side street. He was upset with me and started to let me have it, which, in hindsight, was the right thing to do as a caring parent, but the timing was way off. So I fired up and told him a few home truths—I explained that I was trying to do the right thing but how is a motherfucker meant to be living off $600 a week, for fuck's sake? Then I went on to tell him that I couldn't stand that I was having to make ends meet with this illegal bullshit. He was very emotional and so was I. But Dad, being the champion he is, somehow managed to see things from my point of view. He was really good that way, the old man had been around a bit and he knew the way things worked.

Dad always backed me and I love him for that, he went back home and was obviously very emotional. My younger brother Paul witnessed this and decided to shoot from the hip and have a go at me via text messages, which I despise and still do. Flicking texts to people, rather than having a good old fashioned *tête-à-tête*, is piss weak and a poor excuse for communication. But I understood where he was coming from, considering what he saw and taking into account my history of violence and illegal activity. Paul decided he would stand up for Dad.

Not long after this my godfather offered me a job at his fruit shop. Super Steve Collins is one of the most decent humans I have had the pleasure of calling my friend. Super Steve loves nothing more than helping people and doing the right thing. His wife, my first cousin and godmother, tormented this man with her vitriolic rhetoric, it gave him post-traumatic stress syndrome. Steve continued to do his best even with his ex-wife subjecting him to all sorts of mental abuse. As a result, the great man was highly strung and constantly on edge, but towards me, Steve could not have done any more.

Super Steve Collins burst onto the scene in the late 80s, when I was a young and impressionable kid. He had a flat top like Iceman in *Top Gun*, he drove a Ford Cobra and loved guns and motorcycles. For a young bloke like myself, Steve was the coolest thing since my remote control car. Super Steve took me and my sister Elles to the show one year, it was so much fun. Steve was only twenty-one at the time and we hooned out there listening to 'Born to Be Alive' in the big V8 Cobra. Steve had a habit of spoiling me and I took full advantage of his generosity. We had been close throughout our lives, but I drifted away from him during my sabbatical. It was only through a phone call out of the blue asking me to come and do a shift down at his fruit shop that we reconnected.

Super Steve gave me a crash course in fruit and veg; he looked after me with a decent wage and allowed me to take home a box of produce once a week. Steve gave me the incentive to go straight by putting his faith in me. I will be forever thankful to the great man and he knows I will always be in his corner. This was the chance I needed and from here on in, there was no looking back. Soon I was managing the fruit shop and I became Super Steve's right hand man, trust and respect was exactly what the doctor ordered.

MIKEY

'A true leader has the confidence to stand alone, the courage to make tough decisions and the compassion to listen to the needs of others. He does not set out to be a leader, but becomes one by the equality of his actions and the integrity of his intent.'
— Douglas MacArthur

Life can be extremely challenging sometimes, my cousin Mikey learned that the hard way. Mikey was a gentle soul with a fierce temper. He was a tall and lean man, very good looking with a certain eclectic style about him. He was a deeply emotional human who connected and cared deeply for the people he loved.

Mikey was a teacher, first and foremost. His students adored him. He had his own gentle way of understanding and relating to people. He was completely in touch and comfortable with his feminine side and when you were with Mikey, you knew you had his undivided attention. He made you feel like you were special.

Mikey was an exceptional teacher because he let you work things out for yourself. When I was learning to drive I asked one of my cousins, Zeffa, to take me for a spin. This was the first and last time—he overloaded me with rules and things to remember, my head was spinning. When I asked Mikey, he put his feet up on the dash and chilled out. Mikey talked to me about life, women and parties. Everything but driving and for the whole time we drove together it flowed beautifully. That's the easiest way to describe his style—everything flowed around him.

Mikey's life ended prematurely when a vicious brain tumour took his life in 2008 when he was forty-one. At the time he had four boys, all under nine years old. It was devastating for the family and we were all there when he passed to the other side. He fought a good fight, I'll never forget what his dad, my uncle, said as the funeral people took his body away, 'We have just lost a good man'. It broke my heart. Mikey gave my younger brother locks of hair he had cut off all his boys' heads to put into the ground when they lowered his coffin so they could always be with him. He had even organised all the music to be played at his funeral. I have carried a few coffins in my time but Mikey's was by far the hardest.

I was lucky to spend quality time with Mikey before he passed away; it's towards the end of someone's life that you get a true picture of what they hold in their heart. Usually when people die anyone close to the deceased will rave on about what an amazing person they were. It's almost as if the thought of your mortality forces you to say something nice, even if they were an absolute cunt.

People did say beautiful things at Mikey's funeral and I'm sure they meant it, the sheer volume of people flowing out of the church and nearly onto the street was enough evidence for me. W.D. Rose Funerals said it was the biggest funeral they had ever held and it was an emotional day.

When the tumour was first discovered, my mum rang me while I was living up on the coast and explained that Mikey had fainted while he was teaching. I had the feeling then and there the situation wasn't going to end well. Mikey fought surgery after surgery on his head to remove this tumour. Dr. Charlie Teo, the magician, gave him plenty of extra time on this planet. His aggressive approach to surgery allows him to go where angels fear to tread, he is a fearless operator and we were all thankful that he prolonged Mikey's life that little bit longer.

I was living around the corner from him as the final chapter of his life closed, it was really nice just to walk over and spend time with him. It's funny, with a situation like that, all you need to do is be there for the person, you don't actually have to say anything. It was the last time I felt the Mob was truly there for each other.

One time I went and saw him at the recovery hospital in Brighton with mum and dad, he was in good spirits. So I leaned over the side of his bed to give him a kiss and a hug, which Mikey loved but that wasn't enough. He decided I needed to climb in the bed with him, all 6'2" and 105kg of me in the bed next to Mikey I would have squashed him. So I half lay in and we cuddled and kissed each other some more. Mikey was completely comfortable showing other men affection and I, for one, feel that is a great way to be, I'm exactly the same.

The day before he passed I was minding the fruit shop while Steve was over with the family. Steve rang and said, 'Close the shop we don't know how much longer he will hang on.' So I raced around to find Mikey laying there, half in this world and half in the other. He wasn't scared or worried, he just lay there unconscious, ready to take the final walk. I grabbed his hand and whispered into his ear, 'Mikey, its Jamesey, I love you and I'm here with you.' He squeezed my hand to let me know he heard and that was enough.

I felt as if it was almost like he was transferring his empathy and part of his soul to me.

He passed away the next evening. It wasn't till I saw his body lying there, still and cold on the bed, did I realise an incredible thing about life. As I brushed his hair back with my hand and looked at my cousin it dawned on me that the body is the car and the soul is the driver. Without the soul, the car is nothing; it's the soul that brings all the magic. And in this instance the soul had left, it had done its job on earth, it had completed its journey and it was time to go home.

As sad as it was, the angels in heaven would have had a fucking brass band for this man. Everyone would have been there to welcome home our Mikey.

KOKODA

'This was the place where I believe the depth and soul of the Australian nation was confirmed. If it was founded at Gallipoli, it was certainly confirmed in the defence of our homeland here.'
— Paul Keating

Not long after Mikey passed I decided to walk the Kokoda trek in his memory. My grandfather on my dad's side, Big Al, had served in Papua New Guinea, so I was keen to see the country. The story and history behind the walk fascinated me. Dad had shared the significance of what the diggers had achieved over there. While most people go to Bali in winter, I decided to punish myself with the world's third hardest trek.

After discussing this with my sister Elles, she talked me into raising money for Charlie Teo's Cure for Life Foundation. So it began, I used the fruit shop as a platform to start getting donations and sponsorship and raising awareness around what I was trying to do. The other thing I needed to do was get fit. Bit by bit I had been getting rid of the people in my life who no longer shared my interests and values. And, to be frank, quite a few people from my past started dropping off when they saw I wasn't interested in the dark side any longer. It was a cathartic experience. When you undertake a project like this, without any experience, it can be a daunting task. I was lucky that my girlfriend at the time, the lovely Shelly, had held quite a few big charity auctions. Shelly was a wealth of knowledge, she rolled her sleeves up and pitched in.

Initially it was all about raising some money. Elles, the persuasive personality that she is, talked me into holding a fundraising charity auction. Being a bull at the gate, I charged right into it and got going. Next thing you know people where donating hot laps in V8 supercars, mountain bikes, signed football jumpers, dinners and vouchers for Botox. It was fantastic. I held the auction at the restaurant next door to the fruit shop and all the people from the local area came. The old man had a connection with a band and they came and played for free. How kind is that? Dad held the auction by himself and did a superb job.

The most interesting thing about that evening was the Mob—my extended family—who I don't have the best relationship with. When I announced what I was doing in Mikey's memory at a family function, the reaction was gobsmacking. One person asked why I was having it on a Sunday evening. It blew me away—no 'Congratulations' or 'Well done, that's a great idea'. It wasn't their creation, so they weren't behind it and on the night, the Mob all came and sat with each other in the corner. They didn't buy anything or make an effort to socialise with anyone. My aunt, to her credit, bought the mountain bike and I was appreciative of her for putting her hand into the coffers and producing some folding.

Now all I had to do was walk the Kokoda trek. As luck would have it, the tour operator put me with a group of twelve friends who were all doing it together, that's right, I was the odd one out. I'm not sure how most people would handle this scenario, what I did was keep to myself and just work out what the pecking order was.

For the first two days I didn't say much, I just joined in and helped out where I could. As we got into the serous hiking it became apparent it was all hands on deck. This was one hellish trek. The concentration required to complete something like this is intense. The second you lose your focus, you are on your arse. It's the equivalent of a nine-day test match. On a break I would take my singlet off and wring it out, sweat pouring out. This was one of those moments that you know will change your life forever, because you have this as a platform to mentally bounce off when things get tough.

The country was a lush and colourful place, steeped in history and full of wildlife. The locals have a soft spot for Aussies and that is evident by the care they showed us. From what I saw, they appreciate the opportunity to work and support their beautiful families. Regarding the natural environment in Papua New Guinea, we saw snakes, spiders the size of your hand, magnificent birds like cassowaries or birds of paradise, and some sensational rivers and streams. It was here that I did all my bathing. I also filled my drinking water from the streams, I didn't bother with the water purification tablets—too much mucking around. At night we stayed in the villages with the locals and we got to meet a lot of our guides' families. They performed plays for us, it was awesome.

By the third day I began to open up and reveal myself a bit. The group was also interested in the bloke who had the balls to go one out with a group of friends and that worked in my favour. In truth, I couldn't have gone with a better bunch of people, they were so welcoming. By the last day we had bonded and I had found myself becoming close with a few of the guys.

The guides were all from Papua New Guinea and I got along famously with them, I took a whole carton of Winfield Blues with me and they were all smokers. So at every break I handed around my smokes, the guides loved it and one evening they even invited me to sit with them and smoke joints made out of newspaper—

another case of my past following me. On the last night we got all the guides back to our hotel and had a big drink with them, the old South Pacific beer went down beautifully.

One guide named Scotty was a massive fan of tomato sauce as it turns out. We ordered some hot chips with sauce and when it came out I could tell Scotty had never seen tomato sauce before. So I explained what it was and he couldn't get enough of it, he squeezed a heap of sauce into a bowl and drank it with a straw.

The significance of what those young men achieved over there in the mud will never be forgotten. Outnumbered and inexperienced, the diggers fought their way to victory. If the Japanese had managed to take Papua New Guinea, Australia was going to be next. It was a 'must win' situation. In one battle the Japanese outnumbered us 2000 to our 300 or something very close to that. Once we had defeated them in battle, the Japanese swore there were more than 300 diggers fighting, they were adamant there must have been more men. That is how fierce the diggers were in battle, it made me so proud to be Australian.

I noticed a headstone at the Bomana War Memorial, one kid that had served at the age of fourteen. He had obviously lied to get into the army. Just think about that for a minute, fourteen years old. That is mind boggling

ROCKY

'The stronger a man is, the more gentle he can afford to be.'
— Elbert Hubbard

After about two years of working with Super Steve at his fruit shop, I started to get serious about saving some money for a house and knuckling down. Steve could only offer me a certain amount of hours a week and I was hungry to get as much work as I could. For years my life hadn't involved legal employment and I felt I needed to make up for it. Around this time a friend of Steve, named Rocky, was opening a shop in Ormond and this was the perfect opportunity for me. Rocky is considered one of the premiere operators in the fruit and veg industry. The man is a meticulous artist, with an eye for detail unmatched by anyone I've seen; his son Acorn is very good but not as good as Rocky. Rock is a conservative and quiet man, till you get him fired up. Then he goes right off. Rock is around 5'7" with an average build and a shaved head, Rock looks like a mafia don. He has been around the Footscray markets since he was a young kid. Everyone at the Footscray market knows

Rock and his family, they are regarded as respectable people of the highest quality.

Steve is such a gentleman, he suggested I leave him and go and work for Rock, he actually made the call to Rock and set the whole thing up. So, not only did Steve give me a chance when no one else would hire me, but he also set me up for a job with his friend because he knew I was determined to work hard and get ahead.

At the interview with Rock at a coffee shop near his fruit shop, he told me the work was twelve-hour days, 6am till 6pm, six days a week. The pay was great and the working conditions were fantastic.

I started on the Monday and didn't look back. What started as a job, ended up becoming real friendship. Rock's family treated me like one of their own and I was deeply touched by this show of trust. Rock's dad, Vince, was a hard man from the old country and told me some incredible stories about how life was for him back when he first came to Australia. I now call him Nonno and Rock's mum Nonna, out of respect for the way they treated me.

Nonna was a religious woman who didn't waste time talking nonsense; I loved her straight talking way. She was a tiny lady with a head of black curly hair and a strong sense of her position on Earth. They were kind to me, allowed me to experience their food and culture. In turn I took it upon myself to spend a lot of time with Rock's youngest boy Acorn. Acorn was only fifteen when I met him, he had a rat's tail haircut and used to spit on the ground. He was young and impressionable, so I decided to take him under my wing and show him a few tricks of the trade. I had made a lot mistakes and if I could direct the young bloke towards an easier life for himself, then I would. Acorn was a fast learner and I enjoyed having a little brother like him. Everywhere we went people would ask us if we were brothers.

It was a fantastic time in our lives and I look back at those days with fond memories. The universe wanted us all to be together at that point, so I embraced every moment.

Even all the young kids that came to work for Rock, the local kids that used to come after school and do a bit of cleaning up, became part of the Ormond Fresh family as well. They have all grown up now and we still socialise and go out for dinner every now and again.

Danger was another guy who came into the fold later on; he used to travel all the way from Dandenong to work in Ormond, that's how much he loved working at the shop. Danger was a downright deviant with all sorts of fetishes and sexual adventures he loved to fantasise about. He had some incredible stories. The one I'd like to share involves Danger, phone sex and technology.

Danger was looking through Facebook at these sexy women he was friends with when one of them private messaged him about having phone sex. It didn't bother Danger that his wife was sleeping next to him—he said yes and the sexy woman called Danger through Facebook. For me that is warning bell number one.

Next thing you know the sexy woman has her fingers in the till and talking all dirty to him. He decided to take himself and his phone into another room. When he got into the other room he positioned himself in a way so he could see the door if his wife came in. Then Danger got down and dirty, the sexy woman requested he take his clothes off and get a firm grip on his love pump, to which Danger obliged. Danger was now nude and giving himself a sound thrashing, talking dirty and he had got right into character. It was a tricky situation. Not only was he going to town on himself and having phone sex with a woman he had never met, he had to keep an eye on the door for any movement from the missus. Huge degree of difficulty.

The next thing Danger knows he is mid-stroke and the sexy woman demands $10k or she is releasing the footage she has been recording of Danger pulling himself to pieces on YouTube, with his name and details all over it. Danger turned white and nearly fainted. He let go of his single-barrel love gun and started bartering with the woman. He looked at me while he was telling this story and explained with a dead serious expression, 'This is when I knew something was not right.' Really? Very perceptive, Danger.

The sexy woman was adamant she wanted cash, she sent through the link to YouTube, proving she meant business. Danger managed to get her down to about $500 in the end and after some serious thought, he realised he could just hang up on her, which he did and nothing ended up coming from the experience, not even Danger!

The reason Ormond Fresh was such an enjoyable place to work was Rocky, he was the best boss I have had to date. His generosity and kindness is such a beautiful quality in a human being. Rock taught me so much about business and being a good person. I have always been generous to a fault, but due to my life experiences, I lost this quality a bit. Rocky showed me that it doesn't matter if people take advantage of your good nature—it's their business if they need to treat people like that. Rock explained to me that many people had taken advantage of him, he knew it, but it didn't bother him. He always did the right thing by people and the universe made sure he was looked after.

THE MISSUS

'Sometimes the road of life takes an unexpected turn and you have no choice but to follow it to end up in the place you are supposed to be.'
— unknown

Not long after Kokoda we started to get ready for my sister's upcoming Balinese wedding. We all headed off to Chadstone to look for something to wear. I was super fit from my training and feeling really good about myself. I had put on some aftershave, had my gold jewelry on and I had slicked back my hair. Paul, my brother, was watching and laughing his head off, he thought I was just like a character off *Underbelly*, which is probably a fair comment. I looked at him and laughed at the size of his enormous white teeth, then I said, 'You never know who you're going to meet'.

I headed into Calibre to find some super tight, nut-hugging pants and a ridiculously tight dress shirt with short sleeves so that I could look like Denis Franz in *NYPD Blue*. This took me all of about fifteen minutes, the rest of them walked over to Sportscraft, where Dad was keen to find himself a conservative and cost-effective white shirt. As I walked in I could see him over in the corner doing this ridiculous routine he does when he buys clothes. What Dad does when he tries a shirt on is he rolls his shoulders all the way forward and then all the way back. Then he pulls an awkward face in the mirror, kind of like he's constipated. This can go on for some time and I have watched him do this all my life. So as I walked into Sportscraft, I could see Dad in the middle of his routine, with Mum and Elles watching on in amusement. I could also see there was a beautiful brunette standing at the counter. So I said to her 'Oh here we go, have a look at this' and nodded to Dad 'this could take a while.'

That beautiful brunette ended up being my wife and the mother to my four children. I got to rapping and that's how it happened. I was all over it like a rash; she was overwhelmed by the Issey Miyake, gold chains, tattoos and slicked-back hair. Kate didn't stand a chance—I smashed her with my charisma stick. We were laughing and I could tell there was an instant connection, we ended up talking about my sister's wedding and then I invited her. She laughed at what an insane offer that was, I didn't even know her. But sure enough she did end up coming to Bali. When I feel something in my soul, I just go for it. It's an extremely exciting way to live.

I did mention to Kate that I worked at a fruit shop in Ormond, well she was there first thing Saturday morning with her list, she told me her local fruit shop had closed down—it had, but I'm pretty sure she would still have come if it had been open. I don't like to muck around, so later that day I rang Kate at Sportscraft to ask her on a date, she was thrilled and so was I. We went out that very evening. I don't know what it is about me and first dates, but women were always telling me stories about how they have been hurt and end up in tears. Then after a few more dates these women go on to be raving lunatics. My new rule was: if a girl cries on the first date, I'm going to run, never to be seen again. Well, you guessed it, Kate cried. I couldn't leave, even though a part of me wanted to. But this time I couldn't get myself to get up and walk out.

We ended up back at her flat having a chat; I went into her kitchen and saw a list of meals she would cook for dinner on a regular basis. This was one big motherfucking list and I have to say I was impressed. I did the right thing and went home without making a move, built the suspense a bit—I can be a real gentleman like that. The next day we went out again to the beach, I was drinking white wine to try showing her I can be a real cultured cunt. Then we went out for dinner and I stayed the night at her house—we have been together ever since. Bit of a fairytale sort of set-up for old Hammer Harding, no fucking sweat. Kate told me she loved me on the second date and I didn't know what to say. I did understand where she was coming from though, I am very charming.

We had moved in within three months and we were engaged and married within a year. Then pregnant and with a house not long after the wedding, we effectively got to know each other as we took on life's biggest challenges. It was crazy and wild and not the way it's normally done, but I loved it. The spontaneity and romance of the situation was like a drug. You either sink or swim in life and I'm very confident in my swimming ability. We have had our ups and downs, don't worry about that. But she is an amazing woman and I love her to bits. It's her challenges and the way she strives to be a better version of herself, that I admire most. Kate is always looking at ways to be more capable, to be a better person, to be a loving mother. It's inspiring as a husband and it makes me want to be all I can be.

Now we have four beautiful healthy children. My eldest boy, Archibald, is named after Mark Strong's character in *RocknRolla*. He is a sensitive and thoughtful young boy, very much like his mother. He comes everywhere with me and has done since he was a toddler. Going to watch Collingwood with him and Dad is one of my greatest joys—three generations of Hardings all together. Then there is Lucy, who is a fierce and independent little person. She is an individual and a very capable one at that. Lucy is very much like me. Then there is Reginald, after Reggie Kray the English gangster. Reggie is only a little tacker but he is a strong and aggressive unit. The last is another beautiful girl, Claire. Claire is our fourth child and is named after my father's mother. Dad's mum had some health challenges in her life with alcoholism. We have recently found out that our little Claire is hearing impaired and will have to use hearing aids. As a family, we decided to spend the rest of our lives raising as much money as we can for anyone seeking to advance hearing impairment technology. To us, it made sense.

Having children has been both humbling and levelling, the things they do and say to me is nothing short of incredible. A psychic healer told me once that when I have kids I would understand what a fantastic job my parents did with me and she was right. The stuff I find myself doing and saying is a lot like my parents and it's hilarious.

I am forever thankful to the universe for allowing me the opportunity to meet my wife, she has helped me become a loving and supportive father and husband. It's a different love when you are looking at your fourth child. A mother who is willing to put everything aside to have that many kids, is a selfless woman. So I treat her accordingly. I have heard someone say 'you can't enjoy the sweets without the sours' and there is an element of truth to it. To have someone stand with you either way makes this incredible ride that much more exciting.

2010 PREMIERSHIP

'I shouldn't say this in front of cameras, but it's very difficult to see where we're going to lose a game.'
— Mick Malthouse

After seeing the passion and elation on my Dad's face after the 1990 grand final, I decided then and there that Collingwood was going to be part of my life. It looked like so much fun. Dad walking down the street with a bourbon can in one hand and tears of joy in his eyes. We all went out for dinner that night and I had never experienced anything like that, people were running though the restaurant yelling 'Go pies' and everyone else seemed to join in. Even at the tender age of nine, I could see that the Magpie army was large and I wanted in.

For some reason I thought premierships were going to be the norm when I started following Collingwood, but boy was I wrong about that. It took another twenty years before we would win another one and the wait was agonising. Dad and I followed the Pies optimistically every week through the dark periods of the Tony Shaw era from 1996 to 1999, getting flogged by the good teams with only one good player, Nathan Buckley. Week in, week out we went along. It was always fun to go with Dad, he had a Collingwood AFL member's ticket and he would buy me a guest pass every week. We would get out to Vic Park and the MCG most of the time. Regardless of whether we were likely to win, we would front up and that is what I love about Collingwood people. Kevin Sheedy said after the 1990 premiership, 'I could handle losing to Collingwood, I didn't like it, but I could handle it. Their supporters come every week'. I think that sums us up. You can say what you like about Collingwood, the passion and the fans are real, they may be toothless and all the other crap I hear but at least we are real.

When Eddie and Mick got together you could sense something special was going to happen, there was talk about our goal of being the Manchester United of Australian sport. We definitely don't have the premiership domination they do, but we certainly have the passion. We were no longer the basket case and laughing stock of the competition, Mick had given us a hard edge and we were destined for the finals. As 2010 rolled around there was a feeling in the air— this could be our year. Geelong had humiliated and bullied us in the 2009 preliminary final and we needed to atone for that performance in 2010.

As the finals came towards us, Collingwood was playing some strong football, the players believed in each other and we had no injuries. First up we had the Western Bulldogs, who were no match for the firepower we had up forward, they were nowhere near us. Next we had Geelong in another preliminary final blockbuster at the MCG on a Friday night; no Collingwood supporter was going to miss this game. It was a sellout and the Chief had scored us tickets behind the goals on the second level in the Ponsford Stand. These drunken Geelong supporters were spilling beer and carrying on behind us, just before the game. I was at fever pitch by this stage and ready to start throwing cut lunches. The tempo was enormous and I turned around and threatened, 'If you peasants don't stop, I am going to knock one of you out.' This stopped these peanuts in their tracks immediately—then it began. Collingwood went mad in the opening term kicking seven goals to bugger all and the game was all but done. The Collingwood army went absolutely bananas; to this day I have never seen Collingwood play a better opening half of football. They made the almighty Geelong look old and slow and I realised halfway through the second quarter we were going to play in the Grand Final. We ended up punishing Geelong, I can't tell you how nice it is to say that.

Tickets for the granny were so hard to come by, but the Chief had managed to score Dad and me two seats next to him and his brother up the top of the Ponsford Stand again. They cost $1750 each and I wanted to pay for Dad, to square up for all the times he covered me. So for the two of us to go it was $3500—that's commitment. I didn't tell Dad how much the tickets were. The only thing was we had to go to a Hawthorn breakfast beforehand with Lehmo hosting, talk about a nauseating experience.

I was so nervous; it was hard to look at Dad square in the eye, he was more nervous than me. I felt like being sick, all those years of pain and heartache amount to two hours of football and the chance to taste the ultimate glory. Our normal routine was to have a drink at The Cricketers Arms in Richmond, but due to the repulsive Hawthorn breakfast, our routine was completely out of sync.

Collingwood opened strongly, but we missed some very basic set shots. Clokey was a real choker in front of goal and damn near cost us the flag. St. Kilda was never out of the game and I felt uneasy about our chances. The last quarter was epic, Goddard, the angry prick, took a mark that I will never forget, then he went back and drilled the goal. Lenny Hayes' heroics were amazing and we were just hanging on. Milney ran into an open goal but the ball bounced the wrong way. Benny Johnson was superb and the skipper Nick

Maxwell's save on the goal line was just too much. What a bloody game this was, the intensity was just out of this world and I was finding it hard to keep my emotions in check. This is the sort of adrenaline and high pressure I have always chased. I loved being right on the edge.

Dad who had been at the draw in 1977, when Twiggy Dunne took a mark on the siren and kicked a goal to draw the game, had seen it all before. The siren blew and the scores were level. Every single one of the 100,000 supporters stood up and looked at each other in shock. Nothing but silence in the stadium, it was an eerie feeling. I looked over at Dad and asked him what happens now; he said 'We do it all again next week.' All again, I thought, $3500. I asked Dad if there was any chance the tickets were valid for next week as well. He laughed and said no, son.

I was crook as a dog the week of the replay and I wasn't having any luck with the tickets, this was making me feel even worse. The thought of missing out on going to the replay was compounding the feelings of my flu-like symptoms, now I was suffering from anxiety and despair. If worse came to worst, I would have gone into the MCG and bribed one of the security guards to let us in. Late on the Thursday afternoon the Chief rang me to tell me he had two tickets for Dad and I, $400 apiece. Instantly I began to feel better, I put the call through to the old man and gave him the good news. He was pumped.

On the Saturday morning the sun was out and it was a perfect day to play football. We all meet at The Cricketers Arms and had our pre-game drink as per usual. Mario, the collectables king and die hard St. Kilda man, rocked up with his off-sider Sean and started saying, 'If Riewoldt kicks five, we will steal this.' It's funny when you hear certain things like the desperation in Mario's voice; I knew we were going to win. I was confident anyway after the draw; I couldn't put my finger on why.

The seats the Chief had organised this time could not have

been better—second level, in the southern stand and on the wing. We got there and Lionel Ritchie was banging out hit after hit, 'Oh what a feeling, I'm dancing on the ceiling.' I had the best feeling in my body, I knew we were going to win that day. As the game started Collingwood were on and St. Kilda had no chance whatsoever. The image of St. Nick with his arms and leg in the air, as Heath Shaw snatched the ball right from his foot, is one of the most comforting football thoughts I have. If Riewoldt kicks five? He couldn't get near the ball. It was just our day. When you have a bloke like Zac Dawson on your side, how do you expect to win? We were rampaging Swanny, Didak, Wellingham, Dawes, Sidebottom goal after goal. It wasn't until the twenty-five-minute mark of the last quarter did I relax and enjoy the moment. We were home, let the celebrations begin. Didak had the ball on the wing and the siren blew. I grabbed Dad and hugged him, we were crying. After years of supporting the club, we had won the premiership and I got to enjoy it with my old man. Thanks to the Chief, we enjoyed the whole finals series and that will never be forgotten.

Childbirth and marriage are amazing moments, but this was totally different, this was relief. No one could say a word about Collingwood now, we were the champions. As the boys received their medals and got on the dais with Mick, I felt an overwhelming sense of pride for what they had achieved. There is no feeling like it.

Dad and I walked back to the station together, we didn't say too much, it wasn't over the top. We were just so happy. It was one of the greatest moments of my life. I love to remind every St. Kilda supporter I know of this day; the excuses start straight away.

NO.5 RIBBON REEF

'If all the politicians fished instead of spoke publicly, we would be at peace with the world.'
— Will Rogers

What an amazing place the top end of Australia is. So remote and desolate it really feels like the place time forgot. Sven and I flew up to Cairns airport, Buck met us there, then we jumped into his Nissan Navara for the last leg of the drive to Cooktown, far-north Queensland. We loaded up on supplies for a four-day fishing trip on the Great Barrier Reef, chasing the famous big black marlin. Ever since I caught that flathead at Tannum Sands I have had a love for fishing. The black marlin was always on my list as the most esteemed fish a die-hard fisherman could catch.

Sven and I had only recently reconnected after my family broke away from the Mob and we were thrilled to be banging down the highway in far north Queensland ready to take on the might of the black marlin. The drive was incredible, as we wound our way up the highway. The farms were full and the climate was tropical. Wildlife was everywhere and there were sections where the farms weren't fenced, so the cattle just wandered onto the road. Some of the drivers I have seen in Melbourne would really struggle with this.

We arrived around 7pm and booked into the Sovereign, put our bags down and headed to the bar for a counter meal and a beer. After this I jumped into the pool to cool down and we all went off to bed in anticipation of the next day.

When we woke we all grabbed a few last bits and pieces, then made our way out to the car. I was in the street and was amazed to see the volume of wild mangoes growing. It was only a small observation, but it was clear, we were a long from home. The drive down to the wharf took all of three minutes and the skipper and crew were waiting to load our luggage and supplies. The anticipation was intense, there were so many 'what if' questions running through my mind. We sat up on the second level as the boat made its way towards the deep water. The skipper ran through some fascinating details about his experience on the reef and the quality of the fishing. The two deckies prepared the bait and deck for the day. When we made it outside after about an hour and a half of slow cruising, the lighter gear went out to catch some fresh bait. The baits were mack tuna and they were all around the ten to fifteen kilo mark. The preparation involved in sewing and salting the bait was incredible to watch, the deckies were like surgeons. The size of the bait had me pumped up. What sort of beast could easily swallow a fish this big?

When the light gear hit the water it was game on—mack tuna, giant trevally, huge barracuda, queen fish, bluefin tuna, Spanish mackerel and large cod. It was heaven for any serious fisherman, this truly was the stuff dreams were made of. As the clock nudged towards lunchtime, things began to get serious. All the small gear was pulled in and the big baits were rigged up then thrown out the back. It was marlin time. You could sense the tempo had risen, the crew were all up and about. The skipper was a true professional, he steered this monstrous 43-foot boat with three towers, pretty much with his back to where he was heading. His eyes were focused on what was chasing the bait out the back and how the baits were swimming. He might call out, 'Far right' and the deckies would quickly wind the far right rod in and sure enough the bait would be just that slightly tangled or banged up. This was serious heavy tackle, big game fishing, with the game fishing chair, the harness and the massive gear you see in the fishing mags. We decided the order was Buck, Sven and then myself. Buck now lived in Airlie Beach so he was exposed to a lot better fishing than we were on a regular basis. But when something big started stripping line off one of the reels, the Buck was not impervious to some big game excitement himself.

Once it all starts and a marlin is hooked up, you soon realise the fish is in full control. The skipper and deckhands are all working together with the fisherman to get this fish close enough to the boat to get a tag in it. That's the aim, no long two to three hour fights anymore. The skipper will back down hard on the fish and help you get as much line in, to get the angler the fish of a lifetime. Buck's fight was all over in four minutes, tag and released. But that's underselling the fight. I could tell there were moments when the fish made Buck exert so much energy, he was completely gassed. The fish would up the ante and make another run, then the deckies and skipper would yell at him to go again. The Buck couldn't exactly say no, could he? That is when you need to draw on whatever reserves you have.

Each marlin fights differently as well; Buck's fish stayed down and only came up at the last second when it was close to the boat. Sven's fish was a bit wild, it came up quite a few times and jumped into the air then bent over on itself. This was incredible to watch, the sun was out and glimmering off the magnificent blue water and his marlin really put on a show.

Last, but not least, was mine. As I patiently waited for the big gold game reel to start expelling line, my mind cast back over the hours spent watching the end of my rod tip, on the odd chance I would see it bend over. The hours spent waiting and watching, all the times I dreamt of this exact moment, waiting for my chance to test myself against a beast.

Bang, the outrigger clip went and I could hear the reel being stripped off line. I jumped into the chair, got myself into position and grabbed the harness clips to click onto the reel. The deckies brought over the active rod, then they put it into position between my legs and I clicked the harness onto the reel. 'Wind, wind, wind' was the cry from everyone on deck. So I was into this thing with a ferocious determination. Mind you, I was also well aware not to expend all my energy. I knew this fight may take a while, the gorgeous sun was beginning to set and my godfather was right behind me directing the angle of the chair. It was fitting Sven was with me for this clash, he had been in my corner many times before.

A fish's first run always brings a bit of commotion, still my mind was so clear and it was telling me to breathe big, deep breaths. Then the fish came up, floating for a split second, perfectly horizontal to the water, which blew my mind. It came up again and started to flick its head and throw the hook. I could feel all of this power through the rod and it was the most furious and savage display I have seen in real life from an animal. Then the marlin went on a surging run and the skipper had to back up on it to gain some line. This fish was doing exactly what it wanted to do with me. Now it was about trying to get the fish to see where I was coming from. It's not every day you do battle with the fish of your dreams and I wanted to get it close enough to tag and release it. After some pretty strenuous winding I could feel that the marlin was beginning to tire. The long runs had slowed down and the fish was right near the boat. It still had a little life left and showed me up close and personal what it was capable of with some tail flicking and big lunges out of the water. The deckies drove the tag into her and off it went to fight another day. Such a beautiful creature—built for speed and pulling power, its massive tail and bill are reminders that these fish are capable of so much damage. The streamlined shape of the black marlin underlies its ability to create havoc for any sea creature it feels like eating.

I unclipped myself and got out of the game chair; my body was shaking and sweating like a gypsy with a mortgage. I felt like I was plugged into a power point, my mind was racing and energy surging up and down my spine. This was what it felt like to catch a marlin. I slumped back inside the boat on the lounge and lay there, the happiest man on the planet at that moment. It was an incredible feeling to be that exhilarated and fulfilled at exactly the same time. My life would change forever as a result of that day at No. 5 Ribbon Reef.

People and situations I had previously worried about seemed pale in comparison with what I had just achieved. It wasn't just catching a marlin, it was identifying it as my goal when I was a young boy. The end destination was incredible but the journey is what I reflected upon after I had achieved what I promised myself all those years earlier.

COLLINGWOOD FC AND TREVOR HENDY

'Ego says, "once everything falls into place, I'll find peace." Spirit says, "find your peace, and everything will fall into place.'
— Marianne Williamson

Throughout my life the one unwavering constant, has been the Collingwood Football Club. Among all the activity and action, the one thing that hasn't changed is my relationship with the Mighty Magpies and boy, can she can be a cruel mistresses. Collingwood is the gift that keeps on giving. The passion and undying loyalty that is the backbone of the Collingwood Football Club is important to me.

It's like a massive family—I've heard Hawthorn call themselves 'the family club' and that's cute. The Collingwood family's love spreads far and wide. You could be in the middle of the desert in Iran, meet a Collingwood supporter and it's an instant bond. There is that same passion and love for something much larger than yourself.

We are easy targets, because like magpie birds we are aggressive and relentless. This also means a Collingwood supporter will always bite back and try to have the last word. It's so entertaining to watch Collingwood supporters after a loss, the emotions are extremely high and a Pies fan will be absolutely filthy. For a good while, after a loss, it takes a Collingwood person a short period of silence and reflection to get back to normality. That is how hard we take it.

It's been a privilege to call myself a Collingwood supporter and be part of a massive family. The good times have far outweighed the bad. When my company started to organise the waste management at the Holden Centre, my wife and I were at the club negotiating an arrangement and we bumped into Trevor Hendy. This chance meeting was another incredible thing the club has done for my family. By opening that door and working with Trevor, the club completely changed my life and I'm forever thankful for that. I have nothing but love for Collingwood. It's important to note—players and administrators come and go but the one thing the remains and endures are the fans. I hope the club never forgets that, we are the reason the Collingwood Football Club is so strong and envied by other supporters.

When I was a young boy, we always watched the Uncle Toby's *Iron Man* on a Sunday— the man at the time was Trevor Hendy. My dad was impressed with the way Trev did things, he urged me to take notice of a true champion. So I did. Ever since I was a young bloke I can remember him being a beast in the water, and I loved the saltwater. I remember him doing an ad where he said 'I'll get up and eat fourteen Vita Brits' so I ate Vita Brits.

Years later, through the Collingwood connection, I heard he was doing some work with another bloke I admire, Nathan Buckley. The work was about being the best you can be and achieving excellence from a spiritual point of view, as well as the material success of premierships. Winning from being a complete human, is the way I understood it.

When I finally met Trev at Collingwood, I decided to contact him and begin working with him to be a better version of myself. Trev works on a soul level and it's incredible the way he gets you to look inward to find the answers you need. He has created an amazing program called Bootcamp for the Soul; it is a must for anyone looking to live a simple life.

I have a lot of love for this man. His ability to explain things to me exactly the way I needed to hear them was outstanding. He showed me how to believe in my ability and his ongoing support is a blessing. He's the ultimate bloke to have in your corner.

DETOXING AND SOBRIETY

'I've seen fire and I've seen rain. I've seen sunny days that I thought would never end. I've seen lonely times when I could not find a friend.'
— James Taylor

It took me a long time to find the strength and courage to admit to myself that I had no control over the amount of substances I put into to my body. I would look at other people I knew who took drugs and would say to myself, 'If I wanted to stop I could.' Then I would find myself going to buy some ketamine with the last of my money. On the way I would know what the right decision was, but there simply wasn't a way for to me to actually stop myself. I needed to feel anything but sober; the thoughts of my own voice terrified me. In the beginning it was all fun and frivolity, now there was a need to get high and escape the reality I had created because it was so stark.

Being addicted to drugs and surviving scenarios where you may feel like you have sold your soul to get high is extremely hard to come back from. Parents, families and friends will find it hard to understand why you are drawn back into a scene that is detrimental to your health.

You get used to the lifestyle, it becomes normal. I call it 'the rubber band theory'. At the start of the journey into the dark side your rubber band is tight and springy. The rubber band is brand new and the slightest high or anything unusual gives you a massive feeling or rush. It's awesome and amazing; you haven't felt anything like this before. But you don't notice your rubber band stretching, just that tiny bit more. Because the rubber band is so new it retracts back right after you have expanded it or used it and you feel back to normal pretty much straight away. For anyone with an addictive personality, the first high or rush could be all you need to change your life forever.

You will want to chase that amazing high you experienced the first time. It may be the very next week or three months later. There may be a different drug this time or you might need to take a little more than last time to feel even better than before. The rubber band is stretching just that little bit more and it's hard to comprehend how taking drugs once in a while could have real affects. Then all of a sudden you allow yourself to take drugs once a month, you get excited for that night you are allowed to cut loose and go hard. The limitations you normally put on your body are shelved and the rubber band has been stretched further. It's a lot looser than when you started, but because it's happened gradually, you don't notice.

Now you are taking drugs on the weekend, every weekend. You begin Friday night and follow right through to Sunday night. There are new friends, new conversations about deep feelings you have never expressed with anyone. The rubber band keeps stretching. Some of your original friends may not approve of your lifestyle choices, but what the hell do they know? They're so straight, they wouldn't understand.

Your rubber band is now a little saggy and your body is beginning to show some tell-tale signs that it has been absorbing punishment. The fact is, you need to take lots of drugs to get high now; the rubber band has become a problem. It is so loose now, you need larger amounts of money to pay for the substances and it takes you a lot longer to recover. The idea of not being able to take drugs is actually quite scary.

Next comes the occasional, mid-week catch-ups with friends who 'understand you' and hop onto some coke. No big deal, just a little bit of coke. You have now opened the door to weekday drug taking. At some point this mid-week hobby will become a craving you can't ignore. The rubber band doesn't spring back into itself anymore.

My rubber band had been stretched to the point of no return. I had really put one foot into the zone of no return and I was looking to hop in completely when I had the visit from the Dark Wizard that changed the way I looked at everything.

You carry a lot of disappointment with you around your addiction, for me there was a real sense of loss. You lose your family, you lose yourself and you lose touch with reality. Unless you ask for help and find someone that understands your situation, it can be very isolating. The reality of helplessness and being alone is distressing and leaves you feeling desperate. The need to connect with someone or something at this point can be overwhelming. I continued to take more drugs to keep this emotion from coming to the surface; I didn't want to deal with it.

Some people don't ever come back from this. I have met plenty along the way who never returned. They got stuck, wandering the line between fantasy and reality and that can be a lonely place. There was probably a time where I wandered there too. I guess my self-imposed break from everyone and everything was my time to walk the line. I'm sure there were times that I went mad as I tried to get some clarity and sobriety. I used to run and exercise in a vain attempt to re-tighten my rubber band, after this it became obvious to me how far I had fallen.

This is when I used to relapse—I would be going really well and then I may have a minor setback and used this as the catalyst to take some gear. It went on and on like this for a long time, but in the back of my mind I always knew I was going to get myself clean. I really wanted this for myself and nothing was going to stop me. The need to do the emotional work in order to heal had begun to reveal itself through meditation and spirituality. There were questions I needed to ask myself in order to understand why I continued to harm my progress. Once I discovered I had the courage to ask myself for the truth the answers provided me with an understanding and honesty that I needed.

When you put drugs before your family or basic needs like food, you get to a point where you say, 'Fuck it', and decide not to care about anything anymore. The thought of putting drugs before basic human needs is one of the most harrowing thoughts an addict can have. Even to this day, looking back and thinking I was right there, makes me emotional. I was a skinny, drug addicted human. I'm not really sure this feeling ever leaves you. I feel absolute amazement that my addiction became so out of control. My addiction was so hidden it didn't even occur to me I was an addict until the beast I had been living with reared its' ugly head. Here I was, an addict, getting as I gave. I had some serious karmic debt to repay and I had not yet addressed what a violent person I had become. This would take some time.

HARD CUDDLES

'Cometh the hour, cometh the man.'
— English proverb

After a journey like this, how could I not use all my experiences to help someone else suffering addiction and everything that is associated with such challenges? It wasn't until much later when I began to continuously work on myself and seek out answers to the questions that plagued my internal wellbeing, did it become evident that a lot of people don't get through to the other side. I was an extremely lucky individual, or maybe it was divine grace, that enabled me to endure the challenges I faced and to learn from them and make sense of all the heartache.

When a holistic counsellor I work with asked me how I managed to get through the mess, I was stumped. The truth is I had never given it much thought and the reason for this is I always knew I was going to get through. I genuinely believed in my ability to survive and prosper no matter what life threw at me. So when

I came to this conclusion, the counsellor allowed me to see the strength and power of my thought process. It was an overwhelming sense of accomplishment from deep inside my soul. The counsellor explained that not everyone has the conviction in their spirit to be able to believe in themselves to that extent. I guess at that moment I knew I was going to spend the rest of my life working with men on this exact subject: self-belief and motivation. Not for one second am I trying to claim that I have all the answers to life—far from it, but I certainly know how to ask the right questions to allow men to look inside and make peace with themselves.

There are a lot of men in pain out there because of society's expectations of manning up and getting on with it. Males are living their day-to-day lives with negative thought patterns looping around in their heads on auto play. Men need to start talking about their emotions. My greatest strength lies in my ability to relate to males, anyone I work with normally asks about my background or qualifications. They will enquire whether I have psychology or counselling history and I reply I am a former drug addict and debt collector. My brutal honesty creates a sense of wonderful synchronicity between myself and whoever I am working with. Men relax and the walls and barriers come down, allowing their healing to begin with openness and vulnerability. For my entire life men have always felt the need to share their deepest darkest secrets with me and I have been privy to some incredible breakthroughs.

That is how I created Hard Cuddles, a program that assists men with believing they are capable of living a life that inspires them. With this program I am able to work with men without the constraints or rules and regulations of some of the more conventional processes. Through talking and understanding their emotions men can empower themselves. I ask some fairly tough questions and let them find that they have the answers to heal themselves. Hard Cuddles creates a space for men in crisis after divorce, challenges with addiction and anxiety. What we do is work together on an even platform and discuss the reasons and lessons surrounding those experiences.

It has been said that people naturally tend to hang onto negative experiences we have been through instead of focusing on the most powerful thought in the world: gratitude. The focus on negativity is an instinctual mindset that is linked to survival—if something terrible happens we need to keep that in our mind and make sure that never happens again. What I like to do is work through any negative experiences or challenges, make sense of the lessons and let them go. Where your focus goes, your energy flows. Once anybody has deconstructed the challenges of life, the mind is free and then they can start focusing their energy on the many different aspects of life they are thankful for. When you have gratitude and positivity in your heart, you project that sort of beautiful warmth into the universe and you can be sure you are going to get that back in spades.

Men are warriors by nature, Hard Cuddles helps them discover that power—it's not about being the best, but your best. We address the psychology of fear and encourage men to redirect their energy into doing what inspires them. When you are inspired you are alive and when you are consistently growing as a person both emotionally and spiritually you are happy. The trick is maintaining that happiness through regular practices that engage you with your mind, body and spirit.

Through working with men on an emotional level, my spirit is free. It is empowering to use my story and honest vulnerability to dedicate my life to helping others. No money or material gains come close to the feeling I get when I break through with another brother. Hard Cuddles is the place I needed when I was struggling, I wished I had someone that I could have gone to when I was at my lowest point. I would never have been able to relate or share with someone that didn't understand my language or the struggles that I was facing and that is the reason I created this program. You know you are doing what you are meant to in life when you are willing to do it for free and believe me when I say it is a privilege to be able to offer my skillset to anyone that needs help. Whether you can afford it or not—I am here. I took from the universe for such a long time, this is me giving back.

A CRASH COURSE

I am an excellent listener, that is my gift.
— James 'The Hammer' Harding

I have always felt a kinship with brothers that are at the end of the line: the homeless, heavily drug-addicted, violent, repeat criminals and so on. These are the people that gravitate to me and I, to them. I understand the street life.

I am thirty-seven years old now and am currently working with a brother who I will call the Wanderer. He has a scar that runs from his nose up past the ridge of his eyebrow onto his forehead. It's a symbol of the challenging life he's lived. He is a wonderful man with a heart of gold and an open honesty about his experiences.

The Wanderer contacted me out of the blue one night and explained he wanted to get better. Alcoholism had played a massive role in his life and he had never been able to overcome his addiction. He also explained that he didn't have any money. He began coming to the Men's Circles and listening to other people sharing their stories.

The Hard Cuddles Men's Circle is a place where men come to heal, through the power of connection and communication. When anyone listens to another person sharing a moment of their life that they have found challenging, they learn something about themselves. Everyone is talking or has an opinion on a subject these days, but no one is listening. The Men's Circle takes place at the Carrum Lifesaving Club every fortnight and people from all walks of life have a place to come and be truthful and authentic about what is going on in their lives. It's just that simple. Sometimes we have guest speakers, like the former World Champion Slammin, Sam Soliman and recently we had an old-school underworld gangster come and share his life story, which was truly an eye opening experience. Something about these experiences must have inspired the Wanderer.

Then early one hot summer morning when I was going down to the beach for a swim, I noticed him sitting by himself at our Lifesaving club with two bags filled with all his belongings. He had been sleeping rough at the beach for a couple of nights and the mosquitoes had terrorised him. The Wanderer was brushing sand off his clothes as he dragged on a hand-rolled cigarette made from cigarette butts. Then he pulled out some biscuits and a warm bottle of soft drink from his backpack. The Wanderer had been on his last chance at his mother's house. The deal had been that if he stayed sober he was allowed to live with her. The alcohol called to him one evening and what ensued was a drunken episode that resulted in my new friend being arrested, spending a night in the drunk tank and, in turn, being evicted from his mother's house and slapped with an intervention order preventing him from going anywhere near her place or contacting her.

He was out of options and relied on the Department of Human Resources or one of the charities to organise for him a place to sleep. But now, he also had me. He had been seeing a psychologist on and off, but what I am learning about men is they need to feel they can relate to the person they are sharing their deepest, darkest secrets with or the whole process is a complete waste of time.

I sat with the Wanderer and discussed a course of action that would result in him not sleeping on the beach. Most importantly I showed him I cared and sometimes that is all a person needs. I listened to what he had to share and it came as no surprise to learn he came from a broken family and had experienced domestic violence, which he had never really been able to deal with.

One of the truths I have learnt is that a solid foundation of love as a child is integral to wellbeing in later life.

My new friend had been doing anything he could to numb his emotions and thoughts. He found solace in the bottle and it proved to be his greatest ally and unwavering support for a long time. His health had seriously deteriorated as a result of his addiction, his bottom teeth had rotted and his skin had become an unusual mixture of unhealthy colours.

He talks very slowly but what he does say is both authentic and eloquent and I enjoy spending time with him. He is open and honest about everything and that is all I ask. He cannot afford the service so I have asked him to make truth his currency.

Some of the stories and patterns I see are truly heart breaking and the focus of my work is to show people that it is possible to drag yourself back from any situation in life, any situation at all. The power of self-belief is not sold on Amazon, you can't buy it on iTunes. There certainly aren't any apps for self belief.

With the Wanderer, it is about empowering him to claw his way back towards health and a happier existence for himself. This journey includes a crash course in the force behind positive energy.

What I am noticing at Hard Cuddles is that men have a complete misconception regarding their identity. An extreme lack of self-worth is so destructive that it results in males focusing all their energy on the things in life they aren't doing well. This ideology erodes a man's natural tendency to experience adventure and test himself against the challenges life presents. The fear of failure takes over and men exert their energy in jobs or work that makes them stable but miserable. On top of this there is a complete disconnect with their emotions. Rather than work through these feelings, men choose to ignore or numb out the uncomfortable sensations with alcohol, gambling or drugs. These feelings are never addressed but they certainly never subside and result in helplessness. Some men will do almost anything to ignore these feelings and in extreme cases, suicide becomes an option. Men must shed these harmful misconceptions and learn to let vulnerability, emotion and positivity back into their lives.

The other pattern I come across regularly with males is a lack of affection. Whether men like to admit it or not, they thoroughly enjoy the closeness and connection of touch, and why shouldn't they? There is a stereotypical belief that Australian men need to be strong and reliable. I am a very affectionate person and I hug every client I work with; truth be told, men love seeing another man like myself, covered in tattoos, being so open and in touch with his feminine side. And women should listen in to this, a large percentage of the men I work with have said they really miss the kissing, hugging and touching that took place early in the relationship with the opposite sex. They just aren't able to recreate the magic. A little help please.

The emotional coat of their fathers is undoubtedly the most critical foundation that helps develop a male's idea of how he will form his personality. If a father passes on a coat that is lacking emotion, affection or connection, the son will most likely take this coat and subconsciously make it his own.

The Wanderer was going okay for a little bit and found himself a room to rent in a nondescript halfway house in Highett. One morning, I had this bad feeling in my stomach regarding his wellbeing. He hadn't been in contact for a few days. So I called to find he had been admitted to Frankston Hospital. It turns out the

Wanderer had started early in the morning after he had been paid his disability pension and during the course of the day knocked off twenty pots of beer while playing the pokies, then he took his one-man party and walked through a drive-thru bottle-o, purchased three litres of port and headed on down the beach. He remembers eating some food out of a bin when the police found him and put him in the back of the car. The boys in blue did the right thing and took him to the hospital after his time with them in the drunk tank, where my mate had been talking about ending it all.

Later that day I picked him up and took him for drive to find out how he was feeling. Other than the obvious shame and disappointment that usually follows an adventure of this nature, he explained to me that he was lonely.

He is aware no one wants to be around him in his current state and he understands his choices are the reason he is in this position. It is devastating for him to choose alcohol over health and happiness because alcohol has become the only constent in his life, the one thing that will always be there. He doesn't trust himself enough to battle through this yet. But he will.

The Wanderer explained to me that there was a bloke living at the place he was staying that had done ten years' jail for an armed robbery and had threatened to cave his head in if he ever left his TV on at night again. He had been jumping at shadows ever since, too worried to leave his room. He could no longer live there, the threat of physical violence was affecting his soul and he needed a new place to stay and fast.

As I drove along I wondered if there may have been an element of dramatic fabrication to the Wanderer's story, but I gave him the benefit of the doubt and continued discussing a technique I use involving the strength behind our vulnerability and the boundless energy behind critical self-awareness as we drove to Launch Housing in Cheltenham. The brother at Launch Housing was fantastic and suggested living in a caravan park so the Wanderer would have his own cabin and his own space. Some of the caravan park suggestions were in what I call undesirable areas and even then there was no guarantee of a cabin being free. One of the caravan parks on the list was run by an old waste client of mine, Andrew, and over the years we had become quite close. The best thing about this caravan park was that it was across the road from the beach.

When I made the call to Andrew and explained the situation, he asked us both to come down and said he would be happy to help my friend out with some accommodation. How incredible is that? The universe providing right on cue. What a powerful thing for the Wanderer to observe: the synchronicity of life, how it all connects when you begin to surround yourself with positivity.

Next was for the two of us to go and reclaim his belongings from the halfway house in Highett and I would be lying if I didn't admit there was a part of me praying for the tough guy, stand-over man, armed robber to start his bullshit while I was present. But no, as usual nothing happened when I was there, not a peep from the wannabe hard nut. He just hid in his room and stared at the two of us through his curtains.

As we drove away The Wanderer mentioned he felt the tough guy would get his payback one day and I replied 'He already has mate, this unsuccessful armed robber now spends his days standing over vulnerable people in a pathetic halfway house, not exactly setting the world on fire is he?' The Wanderer just smiled at me. I think he was happy with that idea.

Andrew had a cabin waiting as we arrived. Now the Wanderer had his own little space to call home. I worded Andrew up to let me know if he began to get into trouble and I would pop down and make sure he remained focused.

That is one of the ways I work with people—it's definitely not your average job.

FOREGONE CONCLUSION

'A hard beginning, maketh a good ending.'
— John Heywood

Well, that's the story. It has taken me nearly eight years to write and I hope you enjoyed it and got something out of it. I tried to be as candid and open as I could about my life. As I mentioned before there are quite a few stories and people I couldn't in good faith talk about. Not because of my own personal agenda, more for the fact a large percentage of people I knew are still very much involved. There is also that element of respect for my wife and children—they will read this and I am happy for them to know what sort of person I was, but I don't want to disrespect them by telling all and sundry about some situations that are just not for their consumption.

I have made so many mistakes in my life. Mistakes should really be called learnings. The learnings I make now are a lot more applicable to life and much less severe. But learnings are the only way you get to experience things from a soul's point of view. Someone can teach or explain a situation to you, but it's not until you undertake a learning and feel the emotion attached to it do you truly understand your lesson.

Winning is a fantastic feeling but the emotion is short-lived and fleeting. A learning lasts forever because the feeling is so strong. Mistakes are hard, tough and emotionally draining. There is nothing impressive to tell anyone but learnings are beautiful and inspiring.

My life has been full of learnings—choc-a-bloc. Learning after learning and it got to a point where I started to question whether I was on the right path. I was on the right path, it's just that the path I chose didn't have much to celebrate, whereas a lot of people I have known were the opposite. They seemed to be constantly running to the end zone, spiking the ball and doing the victory dance. I never understood why, then I read something that one of my heroes Bruce Lee said: 'Do not pray for an easy life, pray for the strength to endure a difficult one.' The second I read this my life made sense. I knew I had to endure. Sir Ernest Shackleton attempted to be the first person to travel across Antarctica, he called his ship *Endurance*. His famous quote was, 'Never for me the lowered banner, never for me the last endeavour.' I had to endure all this learning to gain life experience.

The life experience came to fruition when I had a session with a spiritual healer and she said to me, 'One day you will use everything you have been through to help males struggling with the same stuff, you will lead them when you step into your own power.'

Now I use my experience and intuition to work with males, precisely as it was foretold. I had to endure so I could connect and understand the struggle, as Hunter S Thompson said, 'You can't talk about the edge, until you have been over it.' Now I work with males to help them make sense of their struggles and raise some awareness and clarity over the challenges they are facing or have been through. I have created a camp where juvenile offenders get to go back to nature and reconnect with their spirits. It all makes sense now.

I would be lying if I said, I hadn't thought about throwing the towel in and going home to my parents with my tail between my legs. There were nights when I was sleeping on the floor, no mattress, no fridge, no TV, no couch, nothing and I would go to bed starving. I'm not sure if many people reading this book have starved before. It's one of those learnings that never leave you. Up until recently the feeling of an empty stomach would affect me so much, that I would overeat. Not only that, I would eat fast. I would shovel it in. I would have to make sure of how much food there was, so I would know if I could have more or not. I put on a lot of weight, then I would wake up in the night and power eat anything I could get my hands on. Starving was one of the hardest lessons I had to endure; I used to be really skinny and looked awfully unwell. It was only recently that I worked through the emotional content of my lessons and learned that I no longer need to be stressed about food. My lesson was about gratitude and abundance, to be thankful for what I now had and where I have come from and to expect that I will always have enough.

When I started to be thankful for having enough, I began to be thankful for everything and that is a powerful feeling to be contributing back into the universe.

When a person is coming from a place of gratitude, they are unstoppable. The universe will recognise this and bless that person with exactly what they need to be happy. A truly happy person is thankful for what they have and they don't need to chase material happiness, they have this inner glow. Truly happy people are what I call 'Earth angels', here to show us it's possible.

So what to make of all this? I truly hope this book helps someone make sense of what they are going through. My parents had a hell of time making sense of what I was doing. Mum found spirituality as a means to cope with the pain. Mum used to be wound up like a steel spring. My sister and I still laugh at how much she has changed. Saturday mornings were a nightmare in our house growing up; Mum would walk around with her lips pursed like a monkey's ass yelling at us to clean up and get outside and play. Now mum is one of the most relaxed and patient humans on the planet, a real Earth angel, thankful and happy with her lot.

Dad internalised a lot of the material and made sense of things in his own way. He learned a lot about control, or a lack of it. Dad is one of the many who has had some experiences with alcoholism as a kid that made him feel helpless. So naturally he wanted to be in control when he was older and he was for a little while. Then I came along and sorted that out for him. When Dad realised trying to control things is wasted energy, he made some peace with himself. As I mentioned earlier I am forever thankful to the old boy for supporting me through my life lessons, he was wonderful. I asked him the other day if there were times he thought I might not make it and he said to me, 'Son, the cream always rises to the top.' It makes me feel emotional even writing about that. What a kind thing to say.

To my wife, who married a bit of potential or a work in progress: thanks for putting up with me, I know it hasn't been easy for a straighty-180, like yourself. A good girl from a good family, falling for the original hoodlum. It's funny because Mum told me when we started courting, that I needed to explain to Kate about my past. How do you tell someone about something like this story without sounding like a full blown fuckwit? I did try, but the missus thinks she was duped and says to me, 'If I'd have known it was to this extent, I would have run a million miles.' I'm not so sure, I have a feeling the rough life turns her on a bit. She often asks me about my past.

So my wife endured a little bit herself, and she wouldn't have it any other way now. I did the work and got to where I needed to be. The relationship we share now is unique, she gives me the space and support I need to be the best version of myself. That's pretty special and I love her for that.

The most important thing to me now is my family, the strength and clarity they have given me is profound. Engaging with my kids is a better high than any of the drugs I used to chase. These little pockets of wisdom show me it's okay to be sensitive and open with my emotions.

I guess the question is, what if one of them turns out to be like me? Well I have pondered this before and I have an open mind about it. The landscape has changed dramatically since I was in that scene, it will most likely be completely different by the time they are teenagers. So what is the point in trying to forecast the impossible? All I know is—I will be there to support my kids in whatever they decide to try. The only difference now is there is a lot more understanding and knowledge around addiction and human emotions than when I was young.

My great teacher and mentor Trevor Hendy said to me the other day, 'If you don't feel like you have progressed, remember where you were five years ago and think about what you wanted in life back then.' If anyone had told me five years ago I would have five healthy kids, a supportive wife and a home, ten houses from the best beach in Melbourne, I would have signed off on that immediately.

We decided to donate my sperm to a couple we are good friends with, Emma and Tracey. When they told us they were keen to have children, Kate proclaimed, 'James will give you his sperm.' She didn't need to ask if I would, my wife knew I would say yes. If I can help another human being find happiness, then you can bet I am going to do everything in my power to make that happen. So I did the business in a cup and gave it to them. Nine months later Quinn was born. Tracey and Emma want me to be involved her life and I'm more than happy to be there in whatever capacity they feel is right. So five children for the Hammer, I always knew I would have a big family. How beautiful is that?

Temptation is always there for me; my addictive gene hasn't subsided one bit. I have found different ways of dealing with it and it's a constant work-in-progress. It is possible to be addicted to things that are healthy for you. The temptation of making money that way is ever present. Every now and again I will see someone from my past and they may mention a project they are working on. It's interesting because I am comfortable now, but the appeal of big money is something to think about. Sure it would be amazing to have a bigger home, more holidays and flash cars. But at what cost? When you are operating at that level, a mistake can be disastrous. It didn't matter before—I was only responsible for myself.

Now I have everything I need, any more would just be greed and I don't come from that place anymore. I look at some old acquaintances and it appears they have it all: cars, nightclubs, huge homes and a different spunky lady every night. It's interesting even with my mortgage, I feel like I am the wealthiest man on the planet. The gratitude I feel for my lot is impossible to put into words.

The other thing I am tremendously grateful for is growing up in an era without smart phones. Social media has created a society full of pretenders—'Have a look at how good my life is.' It may be the case, but if it's so good why aren't you enjoying the moment, rather than taking photos of your food? I wasn't on social media because I thought it was a wank. But how could I truly have an opinion on something I knew nothing about?

Kate set up a Facebook account for me and I set up an Instagram account and for about three years I experienced social media. I am no longer on social media, the whole thing seemed to me to be fake. It's amazing, the effect it can have on people's lives. The number of clients I work with, that start a session with the issues they have with social media is unfathomable. It's totally unbalanced and out of sync with reality. The ability to hold a conversation with another human is a dying art these days.

Another interesting subject is the cameras on these phones that are creating all sorts of interesting situations for people. Thank God they weren't around when I was in my prime, I wouldn't have gotten away with anything. I would have been banged up in Port Phillip Prison for a long time.

Once I worked out that you don't have to do what society or other people expect you to do, life became pretty fucking enjoyable. My journey has given me the opportunity to look at things from many different angles. What I have discovered is that the importance of staying true to yourself is the most significant thing you can do in life. After all the materialism and glory I chased, I am right back to where I began as a little kid. My focus now is on being in each individual moment as it comes, I let the past go as I wrote this book and gave up worrying about the future. This takes constant maintenance and work, but going with the flow is a much simpler way to live.

The characters I have met on this journey are all remarkable human beings, I have been lucky with the way I can connect with people. Each individual that crossed my path had a story and I made it my business to listen and try to understand them. I can honestly say as a result of this learning I am a wealthy person.

Substances—well, every now and again I get the urge to make a call and get on board. I might hear a song or remember an old time with fondness. Then I think to myself 'I wonder what it would be like now,' but that feeling is short lived when I remember how long it takes me to recover and how poor the quality of substances are these days.

The underworld—I still keep in touch with the King but that is about it. To look back now and to be able to make sense of it all, is a pleasure. I laugh and cry at some of the people and experiences—that way of living is full on. It's not something you can do half-hearted, that's for sure. The risk and reward will always drive a stream of people to continue to go that way. The highs are indescribable and the lows are unfathomable. I hope I have done my best to give you an insight. The underworld gave me the opportunity to test myself against some seriously malicious and manipulative people. I survived and some may even say I was lucky, either way it was one hell of a ride. You can never put these things on a CV or resume, what I have learned doesn't equate to a high-paying office job. But it allows me to live my life exactly the way I want to live it.

I have managed to harness all my knowledge and start a business. It was successful and I found the world of the squarehead to be a very interesting place. Operating in a world where there was no imminent threat of physical violence or serious jail time is refreshing. Collecting outstanding invoices from squareheads was something I treated as a sport, there wasn't an excuse or reason I hadn't already heard. Believe me the squareheads try it on just as much as drug addicts. In fact, they are worse, at least drug addicts have their addiction as a real reason not to pay. I closed that business down and sold it off in small parts, in the end it wasn't inspiring. I wanted to do what I love, which is to help people believe in themselves. To be honest, my family could have lived comfortably for the rest of our lives, had we continued with the business my wife and I started. But the passion wasn't there, it didn't make me feel alive. So we made the call to begin Hard Cuddles and I have never been happier. Working with men is what I was always meant to be doing. I consider myself lucky that I have found my passion.

There is an underpass that my family use as a shortcut to get down to the beach and we have to go underneath the train line, down one steep ramp and then up another steep ramp. My children like to ride their bikes to the beach and after they fly down the descending ramp, they need to pedal hard up the hill to make it to the top. When they get to the bottom of the hill I can feel their little minds dominating their body with self-doubt and all I have to do is put my hand on their backs and they charge straight up what previously looked like Mt. Everest. I purposely don't push them or give them any forward momentum at all, I just place my hand there to let them know I am with them all the way. Sometimes that's all somebody needs.

ACKNOWLEDGMENTS

A special thanks to all the people who supported, believed and helped me find the peace I enjoy today. Without you none of this would have been possible and I am forever in your debt.

To the spiritual healers:

Dalene Knowles—Healthy Minds, Mornington Peninsula (intuitive counsellor and healer)
Denise Bechaz—Clairvoyant, St. Kilda
Tyler Rowe—China Dragon, Seaford (acupuncturist, Chinese herbalist, Feng Shui—expert and Kung Fu master)
Nikki Kuurman—Universal Calm, Carrum (kinesiologist)
Ann Soldatos—Cheltenham (pellowah healing)
Trevor Hendy—Gold Coast (friend and life-coach)
Michelle Mullins—Founder of Aromazen and Aroma Life, St. Kilda (friend and spiritual healer)

Thank you, big love from The Hammer.

To my beautiful mother, amazing sister and determined brother: I love you, even though I dragged you through some incredibly tough times. What a bloody ride it's been, hey?

Dad, you were always in my corner, mate. I tested you on so many different levels and you never gave up on me. You were always there in the background doing the right thing, over and over again. Now that I am a father I am beginning to understand what I put you through and I only hope I can be half the man you are.

To my resilient wife and wonderful children: your dad is far from perfect, but I can guarantee you all one thing, no-one will love you more than I do.

To my other mum and dad, Cynthia and Bob Leatham, you welcomed me with open arms and generosity. The kindness you have showed me cannot be described in words. I am a richer person for having met you both and I love you dearly.

Buckso, a brother from another mother. You're a true friend champ, even though we don't see each other as frequently as I would like. It's always the same when we catch up and you know how special you are to me, mate.

To my incredible publisher David Tenenbaum at Melbourne Books—you saw my vision and took a chance on me. You hold a very special place in my heart. And to the team at Melbourne Books, a fantastic job editing and helping to bring this book together.

Dan Koch, a chance meeting on a beach turned out to be the catalyst for Hard Cuddles and an opportunity for me to watch a true artist at work. You are my brother and I love you.

Rocky, your advice and support over the years will never be forgotten. The love your family embraced me with was exactly what I needed at that time.

Patty and Jonno, two rock solid operators who continuously show me how lucky I am to have you both as brothers. Our three heads together is still an intimidating prospect for all in sundry.

Super Steve Collins, you employed me when I was down and

out, you were patient with me when I pushed you to your limits and despite everything we are still as close as ever. Big love from your pal Jamsey.

John Anderson, my partner in crime. Rehab is for quitters. Only kidding, we rocked it till the wheels fell off. You taught me about life and the conversations we have shared have always been inspiring. When I was at my worst you tried to hold an intervention for me. That's a real friend. Love Hamish.

Matthew Boyle, a dear friend and brother, who helped me to fulfil my childhood dream of tagging and releasing a black marlin and then backed up and got my wife her first black as well. It's always an incredible adventure with the team at Hotshot Fishing Charters, Queensland.

To all the people I have lost along the journey: get the trance music cranking, it's going to be one hell of a party when I see you again on the other side.

And a special thanks to all the people who didn't believe in me, doubted me and questioned whether I was capable. You gave me the strength and motivation to overcome and succeed. The cream always rises to the top.

Photograph by Bill Smyth Images